Making Sense *of* the Cross

David J. Lose

AUGSBURG FORTRESS
Minneapolis

MAKING SENSE OF THE CROSS

This Book is accompanied by a Leader Guide and DVD. These resources are also available for purchase online at www.augsburgfortress.org.

 Evangelical Lutheran Church in America
God's work. Our hands.

ISBN: 978-0-8066-9851-9

Editor: Scott Tunseth
Cover design: Joe Vaughan
Interior design: Ivy Skrade Palmer
Typesetting: Tory Herman
Illustrations: Paul Soupiset, Toolbox Design

Library of Congress Cataloging-in-Publication Data

Lose, David J.
  Making sense of the cross / David J. Lose.
    p. cm.
  Includes bibliographical references (p.   ).
  ISBN 978-0-8066-9851-9 (alk. paper)
  1. Jesus Christ--Crucifixion. 2. Theology, Doctrinal--Popular works.
3. Imaginary conversations. I. Title.
  BT453.L66 2011
  232'.4—dc23   2011038219

The paper used in this publication meets the minimum requirements of American National Standard for Information Sciences—Permanence of Paper for Printed Library Materials, ANSI

Manufactured in the U.S.A.

15   14   13   12   3   4   5   6   7   8   9   10

Making Sense *of* the Cross

Contents

Dedication

Timothy J. Wengert, Gerhard O. Forde+, Franklin D. Fry+,
exceptional teachers and practitioners of the faith

Acknowledgments

I love to teach. I recall vividly, in fact, a week or two into my seminary career, the moment I realized as I watched my professors at the front of the classroom that I saw a possible calling and career unfolding before me. The Making Sense series of books and resources have grown out of that love and sense of call, as from the beginning I have seen them as an extension of the classroom setting I so thoroughly enjoy. Through both *Making Sense of Scripture* and *Making Sense of the Christian Faith* I have been able to engage countless Christians in probing the central elements of our faith, and I am grateful for the numerous conversations engendered thus far. We have become in many ways a true learning community, and I am grateful for all that those who have read the books have taught me.

As I wrote *Making Sense of the Cross*, I was particularly mindful of my debt to so many of my own teachers. While I cannot name all of them in this short space, I would like to acknowledge three in particular to whom this volume is dedicated. Timothy Wengert, professor of Reformation History at The Lutheran Theological Seminary at Philadelphia, was my guide into the thought, convictions, and world of the sixteenth-century Reformers. A scholar of international repute in the study of Philip Melancthon and a tireless advocate for the theology of Martin Luther, Tim helped to spark and nurture in me a lifelong curiosity about how the faith of the Reformers has never been so salutary or relevant as today.

Gerhard Forde was Tim's teacher at Luther Seminary, and so I knew him first—and in some ways best—through his student and his writing. It was Gerhard's treatment of atonement in the two-volume work, *Christian Dogmatics*, that has most shaped and informed my own thinking, and his students will recognize throughout this work my debt to his penetrating and incisive thought. Though I knew Gerhard personally for only a few years after I joined the faculty at Luther Seminary, I treasure our conversations about the cross and admired his faithful quest to understand God's work in Christ ever more fully.

Franklin D. Fry was my first colleague in parish ministry and provided me an exceptional model of what a teaching-pastor could and should be. His passionate and lifelong commitment to Christian education nurtured and deepened the faith of countless members of the congregations he served. I count it both an honor and a blessing that he shared with me the teaching responsibilities at St. John's Lutheran Church in Summit, New Jersey. His leadership in the congregation and larger church is sorely missed.

Two other colleagues, Phil Ruge-Jones, Associate Professor of Theology at Texas Lutheran University, and Amy Marga, Associate Professor of Systematic Theology and my excellent colleague at Luther Seminary, took time from their summer to read an initial draft of this manuscript. Their numerous sage and insightful suggestions greatly improved the book in terms of its content, scope, and structure. I am so grateful for their expertise and generosity.

In addition to these colleagues, several others deserve special note. I continue to be thankful for the support of the staff at Augsburg Fortress, and in particular the exceptional work and friendship of Scott Tunseth, Director of Adult Congregational Resources. A sabbatical provided by Luther Seminary greatly aided me in completing this manuscript, and I want to acknowledge my gratitude to the Board of Directors of this institution for their wise leadership and generous encouragement. Finally, though never fully, I cannot imagine completing anything of worth without the joy and companionship provided by my beloved wife, Karin, and my children, Jack and Katie. God has blessed me so richly in you!

Introduction

Some years ago I was spending Easter weekend with my oldest sister. We were watching one of the "life of Jesus" movies shown at that time of the year and had reached the scenes of the crucifixion. Her then six-year-old son paused on his way to bed to watch for just a moment. As his father walked him up the steps, I heard him ask, "Daddy, isn't it sad that Jesus was killed like that?" To which his dad replied, "No, it's not sad. God used Jesus' death to save us."

I remember experiencing a curious ambivalence about my brother-in-law's answer. On the one hand, it was perfectly understandable to respond this way to a young boy who had just seen a small portion of a fairly grisly episode in history portrayed on-screen. More than that, it was theologically sound. God does, indeed, work through Jesus' death for the health and salvation of the world. At the same time, though, I also remember thinking, "But wait—it is sad, really sad, that people crucified Jesus, and we shouldn't soften that."

Thinking back on that evening, I recognize now that right there in that conversation rests one of the enduring puzzles for Christians about their faith: how should we regard the cross? Is it a sad tragedy that we should grieve? Is it the moment of God's victory and redemption that we should celebrate? Is it the place where we stand in awe to see God's incomprehensible love poured out for us? Is it some combination of these, or something we haven't named altogether?

These are important questions, not only because the cross and resurrection stand at the center of the New Testament's story of Jesus, but also because the way we understand the cross very much shapes the way we regard God. Depending on whom you listen to, the cross may signify God's anger at human sin, God's grief at human waywardness, or God's plea for us to return to right relationship. Further, more than one thoughtful Christian has asked *why* the cross was necessary in the first place, or even whether it *was* necessary. Behind these questions lies a darker one: what kind of God would require such a gruesome death to achieve redemption?

How we understand the cross also shapes how we construe and construct our life in the world. The cross has been seized by many throughout the centuries to justify their causes. The apostle Paul is one of the earliest, as he believed that through the cross God was opening a way of salvation not only for Jews but also for Gentiles. In the century after Paul, countless Christians would lose their lives because they confessed that it is in the cross of Jesus that the true God of heaven and earth is revealed most clearly. Several hundred years later, Emperor Constantine seized upon the cross to symbolize the power of his empire. In the centuries to come, crusaders, educators, dictators, and humanitarians would all claim the cross as the symbol that best explained their missions and motives, even though their various exploits may seem to us as different as we can imagine.

Although the way we understand the cross matters a great deal, and although the remembrance and celebration of our Lord's death and resurrection during Holy Week and Easter is the center of the Christian year, few of us pause to try to understand what it is, exactly, that we are remembering and celebrating. On one level, that's understandable. There are many and various ways to interpret the cross and its meaning. The prospect of sorting through them all can seem daunting. Further, at the heart of the cross is an element of mystery that can't be resolved either easily or entirely. From this point of view, perhaps devout contemplation and adoration are the most apt responses to God's immersion into human life and death through the cross.

At the same time, though, Christians throughout the centuries—beginning with those who wrote the New Testament—have reflected earnestly and often helpfully on the cross. We may grow in and deepen our faith by considering the fruit of their labors. This book is an effort to help you do just that. In six chapters, we will explore together what the biblical witness and some of Christianity's most

---

At the heart of the cross is an element of mystery that can't be resolved either easily or entirely.

---

thoughtful and important theologians have said about the cross, comparing them with each other and with our own experiences as Christians living in the world. By the time we are done, you should not only understand what other Christians have said about the cross, but also what you believe about this central symbol and element of our faith. I look forward to exploring with you two thousand years of reflection on the cross and its place both in God's act of salvation and our daily lives.

Two Convictions

Before getting started, though, I'd like to share two convictions that guide this book. First, I've found that *many of us learn best in and through conversation.* There's something about actively using information that helps us understand material more quickly and deeply. I think that listening to and considering another person's point of view, explaining what we think and feel, fashioning our own thoughts and arguments, and so on, helps us exercise and own the information we're trying to learn far more than just reading it. For this reason, the book is written as a conversation. One of the two voices knows a little more and assumes the role of teacher or coach, someone who has had the time and opportunity to study the faith in some depth. The other voice assumes the role of the student or novice, someone who is curious and knows a little bit about the faith but brings a lot of questions.

It may be tempting to imagine that it is the first voice that is more important, but I want to suggest that the second voice is equally, and in some ways perhaps more, important, as the questions asked and insights offered move the dialog forward. Further, I hope you hear some of your own questions embodied in the voice of this earnest and honest seeker. I know I did, as the questions asked by this second person often led me to think differently and better about matters I've considered for some years. I know that may seem odd, as I wrote both voices. But to tell you the truth, even just imagining a lively conversation about the cross and the questions it might lead to regularly brought me fresh thoughts and insights. And so it's my hope that as you "listen in" to this conversation, you'll find yourself participating vicariously and thereby be more actively engaged in what we're discussing.

Second, and perhaps similarly, I think that in most areas of life, but certainly in our religious life, *questions are as important as answers.* That's not always the conventional wisdom today, as many persons assume that questions betray an ignorance that we would be better off hiding. But I couldn't disagree more. In fact, I believe asking questions is essential to life in general and the life of faith in particular. St. Anselm of Canterbury, whose view of the cross we will consider in some detail, once described his life as "faith seeking understanding." That is, Anselm felt that you may simultaneously believe elements of the Christian faith even while you do not fully understand them, and so he advocated what we might today call a faithful and insatiable curiosity. Along with Anselm, I think that questions are not the mark of an inadequate faith but instead signal the kind of curious, searching, and seeking faith that you find all over the pages of the Bible.

Further, I believe that many of these questions can't be answered definitively. That is, there are many ways of looking at the cross that have helpful elements. So while I'll describe a way that has been most helpful to me and many others in understanding the cross, we'll spend time with a variety of other ways of regarding the cross and try to highlight both their strengths and weaknesses. Each may have something profound to offer you depending on your immediate circumstances, faith tradition, and temperament. So if you are seeking the one and only way of understanding the cross, you may be disappointed. But if you are curious about what different Christians have believed over the centuries and can imagine that many different approaches to the cross can deepen your own understanding, then I invite you to read on and explore the heart of the Christian faith that is revealed in and through the cross and resurrection of Jesus.

Advice for Reading

Two further words of counsel seem in order. *First, don't ever doubt that you are more than capable of not only understanding the cross, but also of letting it shape your faith and life.* Sometimes I think everyday Christians shy away from the central elements of the faith because they seem too complicated or come freighted with two millennia of deep thought. But, honestly, I have found time and again

---

The cross isn't something we just think about; it's also something we experience.

---

that if you are willing to slow down, read the biblical witness, and engage in honest conversation about what you find there and in your own experience, there aren't many elements of the faith that we can't approach with some confidence. This is most certainly true of the cross. Will you understand it completely? Of course not.

I don't pretend to either. What great matter of our faith or lives—whether love, freedom, family members—do we ever fully comprehend? Yet if our goal isn't complete comprehension or mastery but instead deeper appreciation and facility, then I expect that you will find yourself amply rewarded for the time and effort you put into thinking with some of Christianity's keenest theological minds about the cross.

Second, pay attention to your questions and insights as you read. As I will suggest at a couple of points in the book, the cross isn't something we just think about; it's also something we experience. For this reason, your experiences—of faith and doubt, joy and sorrow, health and illness, and so many other things—matter. If I've done my job well, you'll also experience certain things while you read. Some explanations of the cross will seem to make sense, while others don't add up. Some will bring you comfort or even a sense of courage, while others may leave you feeling frustrated or even angry. Pay attention to these reactions and then take the time to explore where they came from. Consider how they help you to understand not only a particular theory about the cross but also the God the cross discloses. Space is set aside at the end of every chapter for you to note both the insights you've had, as well as the questions sparked by material in the chapter. Feel free to write in it. After all, this is your book now!

A Unique Approach

This book has been written as a complete narrative. After introducing the question of why the cross matters so much to Christians in the first chapter, we consider the primary narratives of Jesus' crucifixion and resurrection contained in the four New Testament Gospels in the second. In chapters 3 through 5, we look at three primary approaches, or theories of atonement, used to make sense of the cross during the two-thousand-year history of the Christian tradition. In each case, we will honestly gauge both the strengths and weaknesses of the approach in question as well as compare and contrast them with each other. In the sixth and final chapter, I offer a slightly different way of approaching the question that I hope you will find meaningful. While the book proceeds as a complete narrative, however, I have found that many people profit from reading this kind of material in a group where they can discuss it with others. If this option interests you, a Leader Guide and DVD are available from Augsburg Fortress that may help you in group study.

Finally, *Making Sense of the Cross* is part of a series of books and resources that seek to immerse everyday Christians more deeply into their faith. *Making*

Sense of Scripture delves into the nature, history, and authority of the Bible, while *Making Sense of the Christian Faith* explores seven primary doctrines at the heart of Christianity in the broader narrative of the biblical witness. Resources for all of the Making Sense materials can be found at www.augsburgfortress.org.

I am grateful that you are interested in exploring the significance and the relevance of Jesus' cross and resurrection for our lives in this world. These events, simultaneously as distinct in character yet intimately woven together as night and day, have stimulated, perplexed, encouraged, and inspired Christians for nearly two thousand years. And that hasn't stopped, as God continues to come to women and men through the words of Scripture about the cross and resurrection and through the words we share with each other as we endeavor to delve into what the apostle Paul calls "the mysteries of God." I am privileged to serve as a guide on your journey into these mysteries, and I hope that these words and our time together prove a blessing to you.

Yours in Christ,
David

CHAPTER 1

A Man Hanging on a Tree

I have a question.

I'm happy to listen.

It might seem like a dumb one.

I honestly don't think there are dumb questions.

You might after I ask this one.

Honestly, I doubt it. Questions are the best way to explore something we want to know more about.

Well, this one is pretty basic, something I'm pretty sure most Christians already know.

You might be surprised.

What do you mean?

Only that a whole lot of people going to church don't know all that much about their faith. That doesn't mean they're not good Christians. It just means that they never learned a lot of what you might consider the basics. Or maybe they learned them a long time ago but what they learned when they were kids doesn't seem as helpful now that they're adults. Either way, a lot of Christians feel like you do. They have questions but don't want to ask for fear they might look dumb.

Which means that churches might be filled with people who have all kinds of questions but don't ask and, because they don't ask, don't learn more about their faith.

Not a pretty picture.

Yeah.

Which brings us back to your question.

All right, all right, you've convinced me—I'll risk it. So . . . what's with the cross? What's the big deal with that?

That's not a dumb question at all. The cross is at the center of the Christian faith. Can you say a little more about why you are asking?

Sure. It's, like, everywhere I look there are crosses—in the front of the church, on the top of the building, on the church newsletter and stationary, all over the Web page.

It's definitely a powerful church symbol.

And it's not only churches. A lot of people have crosses hanging on their walls at home; my parents did. And then there's the cross as jewelry. Lots of Christians wear crosses, but so do a lot of folks that I'm pretty sure haven't darkened the door of a church in quite a while. And it shows up in all kinds of movies and advertising, and not always in the most "Christian" of ways. So I guess I'm wondering how it became such a huge symbol.

Good observations, and good question.

And there's more. I mean, it seems like we talk about the cross a whole lot, too. The minister certainly does, especially near Easter. That makes sense. Jesus dies and is raised again and all that at Easter. But it's like we *never* stop talking about the cross.

And you're not sure you understand it?

No, I'm definitely sure I *don't* understand it. I mean, I've heard people talk about Jesus dying for our sins. About him being a sacrifice. And at communion, we sometimes sing a song about the Lamb of God who takes away the sin of the world. But to be honest, I'm not sure I understand what that means. How does Jesus' dying take away my sin?

That's another really good question.

And, while we're at it, I've got a few more. If that's okay?

Absolutely. Fire away. We'll sort them out later.

Okay, great.

So, we've got all this talk about Jesus' death taking away our sins. I've also heard the minister say that the cross shows us God's love. Again, I'm not sure what that really means. In fact, that one kind of troubles me. If God is all about love, why did someone have to die, especially in such an awful way? I saw Mel Gibson's *The Passion of the Christ*, and to be honest, the sheer violence of the crucifixion was pretty hard to take.

So you're trying to understand how a loving God squares with the violence of the cross?

Right. It seems like there are a lot of different messages about the cross. It's about sin. It's about love. I also remember Jesus saying somewhere something about "taking up your cross." With that one, I always figured it meant doing something hard, or bearing some kind of burden without complaining. At least that's the way my dad always used it, especially when my grandmother— his mother-in-law—would come for a long visit. Though I'm not sure that's what Jesus meant.

Those *are* a lot of questions!

Too many?

Definitely not. In fact, I'd say there are even *more* questions to ask and things to talk about.

Really? I kind of thought I was already going a bit overboard.

No, there's lots more we could talk about. Because Christians have claimed that the cross isn't only about sin and love, but also about forgiveness, and passion, and sacrifice, and trying to create an open future when it seems like no future is possible, and whether there's life beyond the life we know here and now.

The cross deals with all these things and more. Which might be why it's such a popular image in our culture—not only as jewelry, but also, as you said, in films, television, and literature.

That's what I've noticed, too. It just seems like the cross is everywhere.

So you definitely shouldn't think these are dumb questions. After all, it seems that lots of people are asking them.

I guess so.

And, I think you might be surprised that, in some ways, they're all linked together.

How so?

All of these different questions get at a central question: who is God?

Wait. I think you lost me. I thought we were talking about the cross.

We are.

So how did we suddenly switch to God?

Because ultimately the cross is all about God.

I still don't think I'm following you.

The cross raises all kinds of questions—just like you've been asking— but sooner or later those questions lead back to God. What was God up to in the cross? Why does God send Jesus to die on the cross? *Does* God send Jesus to the cross? What does the cross say about God, about what kind of God the Christian God is? Is God angry, loving, both, or neither? And that's really just the beginning.

What do you mean?

Well, the other way to approach the question is to focus on Jesus. Did Jesus have to die? Did he choose to? If Jesus is God—which is what Christians confess—then what does this say about God?

And so all of this leads us back to God. Even the questions we asked earlier—about forgiveness, the future, life beyond the one we know—all of these, I think, end up being "God questions" in one way or another.

Does that make sense?

Sort of. I guess I'd wondered about where God was in the mix of all of this, too. I know I've wondered why God would have Jesus die, or if Jesus had to die, but to be honest it didn't seem like the kind of question you should ask. I mean, it seems a little disrespectful.

Remember, there are no dumb questions. And there's nothing you can't ask, either. Besides, this is exactly the question that the authors of the New Testament were trying to answer.

Really?

Really. In some ways, the whole New Testament is a response to the cross. It's just not what anyone was looking for from God.

What do you mean?

When the Old Testament prophets talked about a future Messiah, most people assumed that this meant that God would send a mighty warrior, like King David, to rescue and restore Israel. And so when Jesus showed up, that's what a lot of people thought was happening. But then he went and got himself killed, and killed by crucifixion, which, as you mentioned, is a pretty nasty way to die. No one knew what to do with that.

So what did they do?

They went back to the Bible.

Wait, I thought you said the Bible was written to answer questions about the cross. So how could they go "back to the Bible"?

It's the New Testament authors I'm talking about in particular. Keep in mind that when they were writing, these early followers of Jesus already had a Bible, what we call the Old Testament.

Ah, okay. I think I get that.

Further, when they were writing, they didn't think they were writing the second half of the Bible. They were just trying to make sense of their scriptures in light of what had happened to Jesus. And, at the same time, they were trying to make sense of their memories and experiences of Jesus in light of their scriptures.

The New Testament authors didn't know they were writing the New Testament?

Nope. By the time they were writing, there were lots of stories about Jesus floating around. Some were written, but many more were only being told. So they sorted through these stories in light of studying their Bible, the Old Testament, in order to address some of the questions and problems their communities were having. Over time, other Christians found those reflections—we call them *Gospels*, which means "good news"—really helpful, and eventually they were gathered into the New Testament along with other writings that also tried to make sense of life in light of Jesus' cross and resurrection.

Interesting; and they did all this because they still believed Jesus was the Messiah, even though he died on the cross?

Right.

Why?

There are a number of reasons, but the primary one is the resurrection.

Can you say a little more about that?

Sure. When Jesus died, all the hopes his early followers had about him and for him died, too. The one they thought would redeem them, the one they'd called "Messiah" and "Son of God," was now dead. So when they experienced the resurrected Jesus—or, in the case of the Gospel writers, heard about the resurrected Jesus—they realized God was up to something they had never, ever expected. It took them a while—and I mean a long while—to figure it out, but ultimately they were convinced that Jesus' death and resurrection changed everything.

Okay. I think I'm following you. But I want to ask another question. This one might definitely be considered disrespectful, maybe even a little heretical.

> Honestly, don't sweat it. You can't figure things out in the faith without risking a little heresy.

That's good to know!

All right. Well, here's the thing: You said it's not just the cross that changes everything, but also the resurrection. And even though I don't pretend to understand everything about the cross, I guess I at least find it a little easier to believe than the resurrection. I mean, people die all the time. But nobody comes back; at least nobody I've met.

> I understand what you're driving at. Especially today, there are a lot of Christians who wonder what to make of the resurrection. It's not something we've experienced, and it doesn't seem to square with everything science tells us about our lives and the world.

Exactly!

> There are a lot of people writing some pretty interesting opinions about it. I can direct you to some of those sources if you want. But for now I mostly want to say that you shouldn't feel bad about wondering. Lots of people wonder the same thing today and, frankly, Jesus' own disciples had a hard time believing the resurrection as well.

Really? His own disciples?!

> Definitely. In fact, not one of Jesus' disciples, when he or she first heard about Jesus being raised from the dead, believed it. In one story the women who come to take care of Jesus' body flee the tomb in terror and silence after they discover his body's not there and hear the news of the resurrection. In another Gospel, when the women do muster the courage to tell what they've seen, the men dismiss their testimony as "a crazy story." In all four Gospel accounts, it appears that the natural response to word of the resurrection is doubt, fear, and general confusion.

I didn't know that.

> So maybe we shouldn't be surprised that Christians today struggle to make sense of it all, too.

So don't feel guilty about asking the question. That's the first thing.

And the second?

The second is that the resurrection is, in one sense, *the* crucial part of the story.

What do you mean?

Just that according to pretty much everything in the New Testament, the resurrection—no matter how you understand it—is the primary validation that Jesus is, in fact, the Messiah.

Can you say a little more?

Absolutely. Just like you said, we don't experience people coming back from the dead. And so when Jesus returns, everyone—or at least everyone who believes—sees Jesus' resurrection as the sign of God's triumph over sin, death, and all the things that oppose the kingdom of God. More than that, they view the resurrection as God's seal of approval, of God's sign that the life Jesus lived, the kingdom he preached, and the death he died are all important clues to understanding who and what God is for them and, really, for all the world. So in every possible way, the resurrection is a huge event that causes them to rethink, well, just about everything.

So that's why they go back to the Bible and reinterpret it.

And not only that, but they also reinterpret their own experiences of Jesus and their own lives. Resurrection—raising someone to new life—calls into question almost everything they thought they knew. Which is, of course, why it's so hard to believe. But if you believe it, you have to look at everything differently. And so if Jesus is raised from the dead, then that's where they have to start—not with what they *thought* God was going to do, but with what God actually *did*.

And what did they come up with?

Well, searching through all the passages about the Messiah, especially some passages from Isaiah and the Psalms, they came to the conclusion that they'd actually misunderstood God's intentions.

You mean in terms of God sending another king like David.

Yes. They expected the Messiah to come and throw out the Romans, who were the foreign army that was occupying Israel at the time of Jesus. But what they got instead was a guy who talked about the kingdom of God, was said to be a descendant of David, was reportedly performing all kinds of miracles, and was challenging the authorities left and right . . .

And so must've seemed like a pretty good candidate to be the Messiah.

Exactly, except that he ultimately didn't throw anyone out but instead got himself killed by the very authorities he was challenging.

Which pretty much meant they'd backed the wrong horse. Except for the resurrection, that is.

Right. So now they realize that they not only have to reread the Bible in general, but also to reinterpret it in light of what happened to Jesus.

Because that's what *actually happened*—God raised Jesus from the dead.

Right again.

That must have been a little challenging.

What do you mean?

I mean, giving up your ideas about God, especially when what God actually did was so different than what you'd been expecting.

I think you're exactly right. In fact, I sort of think we all carry around inside of us a little picture of what we think God is like.

Mine probably looks like a combination of my favorite grandfather and Santa Claus.

I don't think you're alone in that. We all carry these pictures around. And they're usually not pictures of a guy hanging on the cross.

Wait. What do you mean?

Well, most of us tend to think about God in terms of what we think God ought to be able to do. You know, God knows everything, so we say God is omniscient; that's Latin for "knows all things." Or we figure God is all-powerful, so we call God omnipotent.

Let me guess, Latin for "all-powerful"?

Right—we define God in terms of God's *attributes*—ideas or theories about what any self-respecting God should be able to do. And when God comes and does something so different than what we'd expected, like die on the cross and then rise again . . .

That messes with our pictures of God. I think I see what you mean.

Yeah, it totally messes with our pictures of what God should be. And although that's hard to get over—I mean, who wants to trade in a powerful, warrior God for some schlep who gets the death penalty?—it ultimately ends up being incredibly helpful.

How so?

Because the God who is omniscient, omnipotent, all holy—we shouldn't forget that one—is incredibly hard to approach. Nearly impossible, actually.

What do you mean?

Well, the great thing about an all-holy, all-powerful God is that it feels like you can count on this God. Right? I mean, this is what you expect from God.

Right.

The difficulty is that we can never measure up to this kind of God. I mean, how can we expect to understand this kind of God, or be understood in return? Further, how can we imagine even standing in the presence of this kind of all-holy, all-just God when we're so definitely not all holy or all just?

I think I'm following, but could you say a little more?

Let me try to explain by telling a story from history, the Christian church's history in particular.

Fire away.

Okay, so there's this guy—a monk actually—named Martin Luther.

The guy so many churches are named after.

He's the one. He lived in the sixteenth century and took everything people said about God very seriously, and mainly what they were saying about God in the Middle Ages was just what we've been talking about. They said that if you want to know God, you focus on God's attributes. God is all holy, all powerful, all knowing, all just, and so on. And the more Luther thought about that, the more worried he got.

Worried? Why? I thought you said he was a monk.

He was.

So what's he got to worry about? He's given his whole life over to serving God.

Yeah, but that means he's got a whole lot of time to think about God, and mostly he ends up thinking that if God is all holy and all just—and knows everything to boot—then God knows that he, Martin Luther, totally doesn't measure up. Because no matter how much Luther may try—and believe me, he tried really, really hard—he still ends up making mistakes—what the church calls "sinning"—and he figures this can't go down well with an all-holy, all-just . . .

All-powerful, all-knowing God.

Got it. If God is all everything, then we don't look so hot. In fact, we're downright rotten in comparison and don't have a chance with this God.

Exactly. Luther ends up feeling that there's this huge chasm between where he is and where this God-of-attributes is, and it scares him. He just doesn't know how to approach this kind of God, let alone be acceptable.

I get that. It's like a kid trying to live up to this overbearing, overachieving parent. Or working for this incredibly demanding, perfectionist boss, except multiplied a thousand times. I mean, where do you even begin? How do you even talk to a God like that?

That's Luther's dilemma in a nutshell. This God-of-attributes—all knowing, all powerful, all holy, and all the rest!—ends up being downright terrifying, because we can never be sure this God will even want to have anything to do with us, let alone help us in our time of need.

And Luther's solution?

That's where the cross comes in. Luther ends up seeing in Jesus another side of God. Or, maybe better, Luther wonders if he'd ever really seen God clearly before at all.

Hmmm. You might want to slow down a little.

No problem. From early on, Christians have confessed that Jesus isn't simply another prophet or messenger, but actually is the Son of God and, because of this, represents God fully. In fact, Christians believe Jesus actually is God in the flesh.

Sounds a little complicated.

GOD ?!

Believe me, on one level it is. Formally, it's called the doctrine of the incarnation—which means, literally, "in the flesh"—and it took the early Christians a couple of centuries to think it all through.

At another level, though, it doesn't have to be quite so complicated, as the incarnation is at heart a promise that everything you see in Jesus really is true of God.

Kind of like the WYSIWYG on my PC.

Now *I'm* not following, but maybe that's because I use a Mac.

We'll save the Mac-PC debate for later. But, for now, what you said about what we see in Jesus being true of God reminds me of when I got my first PC, right after Microsoft came out with Windows.

Which was, as I'm sure you'll recall, Microsoft's attempt to be more like Apple.

Whatever. The point is, when Microsoft first developed Windows, they created this little device driver—a program—that made it so that what you saw on the screen was what you got on the page. Before that, when you were

writing, italicized words would be one color, boldfaced words another, etc., but nothing looked quite like it was going to look when you printed it out.

How do you know all this?

Like I said, this was my first computer, and I tried to learn everything I could about it. Anyway, they named this program WYSIWYG for "What you see is what you get." And it sounded like that's what the early Christians wanted to say about Jesus through their doctrine of the Incarnation: what you see in Jesus is what you get in God. So, in a sense, Jesus is God's WYSIWYG.

Brilliant. Really, I'll have to remember that one.

I'm glad I can help.

So you were saying that Luther came to believe that Jesus shows another side of God, or maybe even that Jesus shows Luther he had been wrong about God all along.

Right. Because what you see in Jesus is what you get in God—I like that!—you need to rethink all the talk about God's attributes in light of what actually happens to Jesus. And once Luther did that he realized that the God we see in Jesus is quite different from the God-of-attributes he'd imagined. Luther says that this God—the one revealed in Jesus on the cross—is vulnerable rather than powerful, approachable rather than distant, and is someone you can count on receiving mercy and grace from rather than judgment. Ultimately, Luther observes, this God is the one who understands everything we go through because, in Jesus, God went through it all too, even death.

Which made it easier for Luther to imagine that this God maybe could accept him, maybe actually love him.

Exactly.

But are you saying—or is Luther saying—that God *isn't* all holy or all just or all powerful and the rest?

What do you think?

Well, I can see how focusing on all the attributes gets overwhelming. But, still, isn't God *supposed* to be all those things? Isn't that what makes God . . . God?

That's where Luther gets stuck, too.

Glad I'm in good company!

Definitely.

So what does he do?

He ends up saying that God is *both* all powerful and all the rest *and* that God is approachable and understanding.

How convenient!

Yeah, I know what you mean; it sounds like a contradiction. But when you think about it, it actually makes some sense.

If you say so. Though to be honest, I'm not there yet.

Try this, then: think about the president of the United States.

Okay . . .

He's regularly called the most powerful man on earth, and I'm guessing that most people are kind of in awe when they meet him, maybe even intimidated.

I think that's how I'd probably feel.

But now think about his kids. To his kids, the president isn't the president; he's just "dad." Whatever they think of him, I doubt they're intimidated.

And they're probably not exactly in awe of him, either.

Right. And that's kind of what Luther is saying about God. In one sense, God *is* all powerful, all holy, and all the rest. You said it well— that's what makes God *God*. But that's not the whole story. That's not even the main story. In Jesus, we also see that God is a God of love, a God who wants to relate to us as a parent instead of as a cosmic president. Luther came to believe that in Jesus we discover a God willing to suffer for our sake, a God who loves us enough to become one of us, to live our life and to die our death. So whatever God may be *in general*—all powerful and the rest—in the cross we see God setting all that aside in order to be *for us*: living for us, caring for us, and eventually dying for us.

Interesting.

It gets even more so, as Luther eventually begins to wonder whether all of our ideas about God are kind of mixed up apart from the cross.

What do you mean?

Well, think about what we've said about God's attributes—all holy, all just and the rest. They make sense because that's what we *assume* God is like, what God ought to be like. And, on one level, it makes sense to talk about God this way, because God is the creator and sustainer of the universe. But on another level, the cross reveals that it doesn't make any sense to talk about God this way and that maybe we were wrong to assume these things. That is, the cross suggests that maybe we assume divinity is about power, but we discover that it's not. That God is most *truly* God when God is being caring, vulnerable, and forgiving.

And Luther got all this from looking at the cross?

Right. Like we said, no one expected the cross. Not when it happened, and not ever since. So the cross reveals a *different kind* of God than anyone expected. Which is good news, because as Luther points out, when you look to the God-of-attributes, all you see is God's righteousness and justice, and you end up being terrified. You can't find any mercy, grace, or goodness there. It might be there, and you hope to high heaven it's there, but you can't count on it because all you see is God's attributes.

But when you look at the cross, you see God revealed as vulnerable, loving, gracious, like a parent willing to do anything to save his or her children. This God, Luther realized, is unrelentingly *for us*, on our side, always eager to draw near to us in love.

Which is why the cross becomes so important—because it reveals to us this other side of God. Or, actually, a whole other God than we'd expected.

That's it. Luther calls this way of talking and thinking about God the "theology of the cross" because it measures everything we *assume* about God against *what we actually see revealed* in the cross. In fact, he was once asked what he thought about when he thought about God—you know, what attribute of God is most important.

And what did he answer?

He skipped the attributes altogether and instead said, "When I think of God, I think of a man hanging on a tree."

What did he mean by that?

That he thought that whenever we say something about God, we should start not with how we think God *should be* but instead with what God *actually did*. That, in turn, means all our talk about God's attributes have to be filtered through a cross-shaped lens. For instance, what do you mean by "all powerful" when you see Jesus suffer on the cross? What do you mean by "all just" when Jesus forgives sinners and dies an innocent man? What do you mean by "all knowing" when Jesus cries out in despair on the cross?

That's beginning to make more and more sense. But I have to say that it also paints a very different picture of God than I'd imagined.

Say a little more?

Well, when I think of God, I don't think first of a guy hanging on a cross. In fact, that's almost the opposite of what I—and I suspect most people—think about. Instead, I think of God's power—you know, the one who created the whole world and all that. But this God seems pretty powerless. Is that what Luther meant by saying we have to filter talk about God's attributes through the cross?

That's exactly what he meant. His "theology of the cross" means calling into question our assumptions about God, including how God is powerful.

How **God is powerful? What do you mean?**

The cross invites—maybe actually demands—that we reconsider what we assumed about God and God's power in light of what God actually did in Jesus. So the question becomes, what does God's power look like when it doesn't come packaged as a mighty king or warrior but instead is revealed in a guy who gets executed?

So Luther—and lots of other Christians, too, I'm assuming—focused on the cross because it told him things he might have missed otherwise?

Right. In fact, one of my favorite movies with lots of cross imagery sums it up pretty well.

What's the movie?

Cool Hand Luke.

I've heard of it—the one with Paul Newman, right?—but haven't seen it.

It's about this guy named Luke, obviously, who doesn't understand life. He's come back from a war and nothing makes sense, so he starts doing stupid things, like cutting the heads off of parking meters.

Why does he do that?

You don't really know, except that, in general, the rules of society don't make sense to him—whether they're big rules like why you have to go to jail for committing a crime, or little ones like why you have to pay to park your car. In any event, because of the stuff he's doing, he ends up in jail.

And there are lots of rules in jail, too, but they don't make sense to him, either. So he breaks them, and he gets punished. And he breaks more and is punished more, until he finally tries to escape prison. When he's brought back, the prison warden says, "What we've got here is a failure to communicate." And that pretty much sums things up—it's like someone forgot to communicate to Luke something important about life, and so none of it makes sense.

And this connects to the cross . . . how?

I think that's what Luther is trying to say about our life of faith, too. Apart from the cross, all we can imagine is the God-of-attributes, and so God ends up being kind of terrifying and much of life doesn't make sense.

There's this great scene in the movie when a thunderstorm comes up. The other prisoners run to take shelter, but Luke just stays out there and starts yelling up at the thunder and lightning, eventually shouting at the all-powerful God one of the other prisoners is afraid of. Except Luke's not sure this God even exists, so he shouts, "Let me know you're up there. Come on. Love me, hate me, kill me, anything. Just let me know it." Finally, he gives up. The God-of-attributes either doesn't exist or is just not approachable.

I think I see what you mean. So Luther is saying that we're like Luke: most of life, and definitely God, doesn't make a whole lot of sense unless you have a clearer sense of not just *what* God is, but *who* God is.

Right! And according to Luther, if much of life feels like a failure to communicate, then the cross is God's way of establishing communication, of telling us more directly what God is up to and just who God really is for us.

Okay, I think I'm with you, more or less, with an emphasis on *think*.

I know what you mean; it takes a little time for it to sink in. But this is exactly why your questions are such good ones and why the cross is worth talking about. Because it's right at the center of the Christian faith and, as we've already seen, not the simplest thing to explain or understand.

You're telling me.

Like I said, it took the earliest Christians, the ones who wrote what we call the New Testament, a long time to think all this through.

How long, exactly?

A couple of generations, at least. Maybe it will help if I give you a general timeline.

I'll take it.

Okay, so the earliest writings we have in the New Testament come from the apostle Paul, an early convert to Christianity who spread the message of Jesus throughout the ancient world.

Paul—he's the one who wrote all the letters?

That's right.

And what's an "apostle"?

It comes from a Greek word. It means "one who is sent with a message." And that's Paul in a nutshell. He was a missionary pastor, called and commissioned to share the message of Jesus with as many people as possible. So after getting a new Christian community started, he would usually move on to a new territory where people hadn't heard the gospel yet. Often, though, the communities he had founded would write him for advice, and many of the letters we have in the New Testament are his responses to some of these questions.

Got it.
But I have to say this surprises me a bit. I mean, I'm sure Paul's letters are important, but I really would have guessed that the four Gospels came first. After all, they're the stories about Jesus.

That's completely understandable. I think most of us grew up assuming the Gospels were written first. But they actually come much later, about forty to fifty years after Jesus taught his disciples. On the other hand, Paul was writing only about twenty years later.

Why do the Gospels come so much later?

Lots of reasons: the early Christians were busy spreading the news. They thought Jesus might return soon so there didn't seem to be any need to write things down, there were plenty of eye-witnesses around to tell the stories, and so on. But after a while, when they realized Jesus wasn't coming right back, and because some of the eye-witnesses were dying, it suddenly seemed like a good idea to collect the stories, sort through them, and tell them in a way that could help new Christians understand the ministry and mission of Jesus.

Interesting.

Further, they probably weren't written by eye-witnesses. Luke, one of the people who wrote a Gospel, says as much at the very beginning of his book; he says that there are a lot of stories about Jesus floating around that have been passed down by actual eye-witnesses, and he's now trying to sort through them and put together an ordered account for his community.

I never knew that, either.

Again, you're not alone. But, to put it simply, the apostle Paul comes first, as he's writing in the early fifties of the first century, or about twenty years after Jesus died. Then come the four Gospels—probably Mark first, around 70, near when the Romans destroyed the temple of Jerusalem. Then Luke and Matthew followed ten or so years after that, and finally the Gospel of John was written, maybe another decade or so later, around 90 or so, or nearly sixty years after Jesus' actual ministry.

And all this time they're trying to figure out the cross?

Right, and what's interesting is that as you go from Paul to John you can actually see the early Christians' understanding of the cross develop.

What do you mean?

Nearly all of what Paul says about Jesus centers on Jesus' cross and resurrection, how that changes everything.

Like we do in church.

Sort of, but it's more than that. I mean, Paul talks about all kinds of things—ethics, church divisions, local customs. But everything he takes up he discusses in light of the cross. Interestingly, he says next to nothing about Jesus' actual life. In fact, it's hard to know if he even knows anything about Jesus' life and ministry.

What do you mean?

Well, Paul doesn't tell any stories about Jesus—no miracles, no parables, no sermons, nothing. So if he knows them, he obviously doesn't think they're important, because all he does is talk about the difference the cross and resurrection make.

So where do all the stories come from then?

They come from the eyewitnesses and traditions about Jesus Luke mentions, and they end up getting written down in the Gospels, connected to the story of the cross.

So they've realized, like you said earlier, that the cross helps them understand all the stories they have about Jesus' life.

Right, but here's where it gets even more interesting. Mark, who writes first, begins his story with Jesus' baptism. Matthew and Luke, writing ten years or so later, begin their stories with Jesus' birth. Then John, writing still another decade later, begins his story of Jesus at the very beginning of time, starting his Gospel with a line that echoes the beginning of Genesis: "In the beginning was the Word."

So if Paul is writing in the 50s and only talks about the cross, and John is writing, what, about forty years later, and has taken that story all the way back to the beginning of time, it's like the longer they have to think about Jesus' cross the more it explains for them.

Exactly—first it's just the cross and resurrection. Then Mark uses the cross and resurrection to make sense of Jesus' ministry and all the stories about him. Then Matthew and Luke realize . . . no, wait, this helps us understand his birth, too. And then John comes along and says, sorry, but we're not done yet—the cross has implications for all of human history.

That's pretty cool. I can see why they'd take a long time to think all this through. And, clearly, it doesn't stop there. Like you said, Luther is still thinking about all this fifteen hundred years later, and we're still thinking it through today.

Absolutely. And what all of these conversations have in common is that they all center on figuring out what God is up to in the cross, about what the cross tells us about God. Not about *what* God is—all powerful and the rest—but instead, about *who* God is for us.

Interesting.

I think so, too.

Okay, that helps me understand why the cross becomes so important to the early Christians and, for that matter, to Christians ever since. It tells us

something about God, something we didn't expect, something that changes the way we think about God and, I suppose, everything else, too. That makes sense.

But we're still a long way from answering all the other questions I mentioned, about what the cross means and how it relates to sin and forgiveness and all the rest.

You're absolutely right. We've just scratched the surface. Where do you want to begin?

To be honest, my head is spinning a bit with all the questions I have. But I think at this point I am most curious about what you said about the whole New Testament being a response to the cross, and I find it really interesting how much the thought of the authors of the New Testament developed while it was being written.

Yeah, it is interesting, and it's also part of what makes the cross so challenging for us to understand today.

What do you mean?

Well, like I said, it takes a while, and just as Paul and the four Gospel writers start at different places in terms of how far back they go with Jesus' story in light of the cross, they don't all end up at the same place, either.

I'm not sure I'm following.

Well, we'd like to think there's one and only one way to interpret the cross, but in the New Testament there are actually several different interpretations. What Paul thinks isn't exactly the same as Mark, and that's not the same as John, and we haven't even talked about some of the other letters and documents in the New Testament. As it turns out, there are several different ways to answer the question: what is God up to in the cross?

That sounds like it could get confusing, especially if the Gospels are saying totally different things about the cross.

I don't think I'd go so far as to say they're saying *totally* different things. They definitely tell a similar story and overlap in lots of places, but no question about it, they also have different emphases.

Can you say a little more?

Each Gospel has a particular point of view it's trying to get across, a distinct confession of faith about Jesus that is addressed to different Christian communities that were facing different challenges and asking different questions. As you said, this can get complicated, even problematic. So much so that one early Christian leader blended the four together into one seamless story.

Sounds like a reasonable solution.

Maybe. I mean, it was definitely popular for some time in some parts of the early Christian world, but after a while most Christians actually appreciated having four distinct stories about Jesus.

Why? Wouldn't they rather have one clear story instead of four different ones?

I think they ended up feeling like you lose too much when you splice them all together. Maybe having four stories, each with a distinct perspective, gets a little complicated at times, but in the end, the early Christians figured that what God was doing in Jesus to save us and all the world was, well, complex. And they believed that somehow you get a richer, truer picture of Jesus through the four different perspectives than you do by slapping them all together into one.

Kind of like when I was at an art museum once and was looking at this statue on the museum lawn. Each time I moved, it looked a little different. I saw different angles and contours; the lighting was a little different, and so forth. I ended up seeing all kinds of details that I would have missed if I'd seen it from just one angle, like in a picture.

That's a great illustration—the four Gospels give us a more three-dimensional view of what God is doing in Jesus. That makes things a little more complicated at times, but it also makes it much more interesting.

By the time I was done walking around the statue, I felt like I'd really seen it.

And that's what the early Christians felt like, too. The distinct but complimentary perspectives on Jesus give us a more complete and true picture of what God is doing in Jesus, especially through his cross and resurrection. Each Gospel, that is, tries to show us something about God that maybe we hadn't noticed before, something about how God is *for us* that the cross makes clear.

It sounds like each Gospel presents its own theology of the cross. So maybe that's where we should go now, to look at the way each of the Gospels describes what's going on in the cross.

Sounds like a plan. Let's go there next.

Insights and Questions

CHAPTER **2**

Portraits and Perspectives

So you said that the four Gospel accounts offer complimentary but distinct pictures of Jesus and, in particular, of the cross.

Yes. And I really liked your comparison of the four Gospels to looking at a work of art from different angles, each one emphasizing different attributes of the sculpture so that, taken together, you have a richer, more three-dimensional view.

Thanks.

You're welcome. It occurred to me that a similar way to think about it might be to imagine four talented artists painting the same scene or person. You can see the resemblance between the paintings because the subject is the same, but each portrait offers a different perspective, focusing on something deeply true that only that artist sees.

Yeah, I like that one, too.

It also underscores what's going on in the Gospels; really, in the Bible more generally.

What do you mean?

The authors of the Bible didn't imagine themselves writing history as we think of it today. Instead, they were offering various portraits and distinct confessions of faith. They wanted to report what Jesus did, but they really wanted to show who Jesus is and why his life, death, and resurrection matter. They also wanted their confessions to *do* something.

I'm not sure what you mean. How does a story do something?

Good stories make an impact on us. They affect how we think and act. The Gospels are no different. In fact, they are primarily intended to persuade us of the truth they confess so that we actually shape our lives around the truth.

So they wanted to emphasize the meaning of Jesus' life, not just report some facts. That makes sense. I read somewhere that in the ancient world "history" was more about trying to make a point, persuade people of the truth about something. It was far more than recording things with factual accuracy, the way we do today.

That's right. Furthermore, the four Gospel writers were not offering these confessions in general but to specific communities of faith. And so each Gospel starts with a particular group of Christians in mind and tries to tell the story in a way that makes sense to them, while also addressing some of the particular concerns, problems, and setbacks that specific community was having.

For instance?

Well, it's widely thought that Mark's community was undergoing or had recently emerged from persecution of some kind, while some think John's community was largely made up of people who had been quarreling with other Jews or who even had been recently expelled from a local synagogue. Similarly, while Matthew's community probably included mostly Jewish believers who were trying to understand how Jesus was the Messiah they were hoping for, Luke's people represented a variety of cultural and religious backgrounds.

And all of this stuff shaped how they painted the Gospel portraits we now have.

Exactly. And keeping all this in mind is helpful, especially when we notice some of the differences between the four accounts.

And how big are these differences you're talking about?

Some are pretty small, like whether the disciples fell asleep only once the night before Jesus' crucifixion, as in Luke, or three times, as in Mark and Matthew. Others are a lot bigger, like did Jesus die on the day of Passover or the day before Passover? Whatever the differences, if we just remember that the Gospels are distinct confessions of faith offering their own perspectives on a larger truth, then we don't need to get worried when we come across discrepancies in the stories or try to make them all fit.

That actually makes a lot of sense. In fact, it seems like we could learn a lot from paying attention to the differences.

Absolutely. Each difference we encounter functions like a clue to the meaning of the larger story the author is trying to tell. So when we come across a difference between, for instance, Luke and Mark, the question isn't, "Which one is right?" but instead, "What's Luke trying to tell us with this different detail?"

That's helpful and definitely worth remembering. Okay, where should we start?

I think we'll appreciate the differences in the Gospels even more if we start with at least one overarching similarity shared by all four of them. It might seem obvious given what we talked about earlier, but it's still really important.

What's that?

Each of these four stories totally revolves around the cross.

I guess that figures. After all, that's where we started, with how the cross is everywhere. But when it comes to the actual books in the New Testament, I thought you said earlier that it's Paul's letters that are totally about the cross, and the Gospels give us all of the other stories about Jesus.

That's true. But all of the Gospels' stories about Jesus' teaching and miracles and even his birth point to the cross.

What do you mean?

Well, take the birth stories that Matthew and Luke tell. Each one has elements that help prepare us for the cross at the end of the story.

Like foreshadowing in a good novel, when a character has a dream or something and it gives you an idea of something that will happen later?

Exactly. In Matthew, for example, you have the story about Herod, the local political authority. When he hears that the "king of the Jews" is about to be born, he consults with the chief priests and scribes—the religious authorities—to figure out where Jesus is supposed to be born. And then, when he can't find Jesus, he kills all the male babies in that area just to make sure he gets Jesus.

That's terrible. I don't remember hearing that story.

It is an awful story, so not everyone wants to read it.

What happened to Jesus?

His father was warned by an angel to flee to Egypt, so they got away safely.

And this is the foreshadowing we were talking about—Herod trying to kill Jesus at the very beginning of his life?

Right. Because at the end of the story another political leader, Pontius Pilate, conspires with chief priests, Pharisees, and scribes—the religious leaders—to put Jesus to death. Even from his birth, Matthew says, Jesus instilled fear in people, and they wanted to kill him.

I see what you mean.

Luke also uses foreshadowing in telling his story. When Jesus' parents, Mary and Joseph, bring Jesus to the temple for his naming—which happens eight days after birth in Jewish tradition—they meet an old man named Simeon who prophesies about Jesus' destiny as the Messiah.

What does he say?

He says lots of good things about Jesus being a light to many nations and the one who will restore the glory of Israel.

Which makes sense, because as you said, Luke is addressing a community made up not only of Jewish believers but persons from all different religious backgrounds.

> Right. But Simeon also says that Jesus is "destined for the falling and the rising of many in Israel, and to be a sign that will be opposed," and then he looks right at Mary and says, "and a sword will pierce your own soul too" (Luke 2:34-35).

That's pretty chilling.

> Yeah, it really is, and that's the point—from his very birth you knew there was trouble waiting. And these kinds of clues are everywhere in the Gospels. For instance, in Matthew, Mark, and Luke, Jesus predicts his death and resurrection three times.

Three times? Like once wasn't enough to get everyone's attention?

> Apparently not. But that's part of the story, too: no one expects the cross, not even when Jesus predicts it. Some of his parables and other teachings also point ahead to his rejection and crucifixion, but again no one sees it coming.

So I'm beginning to see what you mean about the cross being everywhere. Even if there are all these other stories, they are all still, in one way or another, about the cross.

> That's right. One biblical scholar said that reading Mark was like reading a passion narrative—a story about the cross—with a long introduction. In fact, about one-third of Mark's story is about the last week of Jesus' life. That's true of half of John's Gospel, too.

So a passion story with a long introduction seems to pretty well sum it up. But does that mean that the cross is the only thing that matters in the Gospels?

> Great question. The cross is central, as it's the place where these early Christians believed they saw God doing a new thing, being available for them in a new way. But the very nature of the Gospels shows that Jesus' whole life matters.

Can you say a little more?

Sure. As much as the Gospels focus on the cross, they tell the *whole* story of Jesus' life. So it's like they're saying that you can't really understand the cross without understanding his life—that is, by paying attention to the kind of life he lived and why people want to put him to death. At the same time, you can't understand his life apart from the cross—that is, this isn't just the story of one good man who challenged the status quo; it's the story of how God worked in and through Jesus' life and ministry not just to care for the world but actually to redeem it.

So we need to think about what Jesus' life says about his cross and what the cross tells us about his life?

Right. Ultimately, all of the Gospels are trying to show their readers how it is that we not only see God more clearly because of Jesus' life and death, but also how God meets them in and through their own suffering as they try to follow the life Jesus led.

Makes sense, although to be honest, it's a lot to get my head around.

You're absolutely right. But I think all of this will get clearer as we turn to look at the distinct confession of each Gospel and see how each writer was trying to point to God's ongoing activity through his story of Jesus' life, death, and resurrection.

Sounds good. Where should we start?

Let's begin with Mark.

Oh, right, because you said that Mark was probably the first Gospel written.

Right. We can tell this from some of the references Mark makes to the Temple in Jerusalem that was destroyed by the Romans in A.D. 70, and from the fact that Luke and Matthew both seem to rely on Mark heavily for their accounts. This implies that they had a copy of Mark with them when they wrote.

Okay, so what's Mark's take on the cross?

Well, there are a couple of things that stand out. But rather than just name them, I think we'll appreciate Mark's theology more if we look closely at a few parts of Mark's actual story and see them in action.

Kind of like looking at some of the details of a portrait—like we talked about earlier—first-hand. That makes sense.

Good. While it would be best to read the whole of Mark's Gospel, we can save a little time and start with a brief overview of the scenes in Mark's story. This will help us follow Mark's story better and also provide a good backdrop against which to read the other Gospels.

Scenes? You make it sound like a play.

Well, it is very much a drama, and the Gospel writers are very much artists, as we've been saying, so "scenes" works well as a way of thinking about the movement of Mark's story.

Got it.

Mark arranges his passion narrative into five scenes.

Passion narrative?

The part of a Gospel that focuses on Jesus' crucifixion and the events right before it happens.

Okay.

Here's a general outline of key events in Mark's Gospel:
- Jesus shares a last supper with his disciples (14:12-31).
- After this meal, Jesus goes with them to the Garden of Gethsemane where he prays and then is betrayed (14:32-52).
- He is first taken to be questioned by the religious authorities (14:53-72).
- Next he goes in front of Pontius Pilate, the Roman political authority (15:1-15).
- Then he is crucified, dies, and is buried (15:16-47).

And the other Gospels follow this same outline?

More or less. Any variations on this order are things we'll want to pay attention to.

What about the resurrection? You said that was important, too.

It's very important. And each of the Gospel writers describes that quite differently, sometimes in several scenes all his own. So we'll talk about that as well, but we'll treat it as a distinct episode that comes after the passion story.

All right. I think I'm with you.

Great. So let's start with the scene in Gethsemane.

Not the last supper?

The last supper is, of course, important to the Gospel stories and to Christian worship today, but with Mark I think I'd like to start in Gethsemane, the place Jesus goes to pray with his disciples and where his opponents come to find him.

Okay.

Let's look at this scene together and you can tell me what you notice.

Wait a second—I thought you were explaining this to me!

I'm definitely here to help, but anyone can read and understand the Bible. The key is treating it like any other good story you'd read by slowing down and noticing the details. So that's what I want you to do. Just listen to it like a story, and then tell me what sticks out to you, what details of Mark's carefully crafted drama make an impression.

Okay, I'll give it a try.

Great. Here it is:

> *They went to a place called Gethsemane; and he said to his disciples, "Sit here while I pray." He took with him Peter and James and John, and began to be distressed and agitated. And he said to them, "I am deeply grieved, even to death; remain here, and keep awake." And going a little farther, he threw himself on the ground and prayed that, if it were possible, the hour might pass from him. He said, "Abba, Father, for you all things are possible; remove this cup from me; yet, not what I want, but what you want." He came and found them sleeping; and he said to Peter, "Simon, are you asleep? Could you not keep awake one hour? Keep awake and pray that you may not come into the time of trial; the spirit indeed is willing, but the flesh is weak." And again he went away and prayed, saying the same*

words. And once more he came and found them sleeping, for their eyes were very heavy; and they did not know what to say to him. He came a third time and said to them, "Are you still sleeping and taking your rest? Enough! The hour has come; the Son of Man is betrayed into the hands of sinners. Get up, let us be going. See, my betrayer is at hand." (14:32-42)

Well, the first thing that sticks out to me was just how vividly Mark describes Jesus' fear about what's going to happen. I generally don't think of Jesus getting agitated. Most of the pictures you see in churches portray Jesus as so calm and serene, like nothing could ever bother him, but here he seems not just afraid, but downright upset.

Yes, I think that's true.

It makes Jesus seem so, I don't know, *human*. I'm not sure if that's the best way to describe it, but it's definitely the word that comes to mind.

I actually think that's a pretty good word, and it's one I've heard a lot of folks use when they read Mark.

And is this one of the distinctive parts of Mark's story?

It definitely contrasts, as we'll see, with John, where he looks a lot more like the pictures in churches—always calm, cool, and collected.

So why does Mark tell it this way?

Well, let's start with your own reactions. How does this portrayal make you feel about Jesus?

Like I said, it makes him seem very human, so I guess it means I can identify with him as a character. It also makes me wonder if at this moment he's full of doubts, like maybe he wonders if he made a big mistake, if God really can save him. Again, this is all stuff I can identify with.

Right. So keep in mind that Mark, as I said, was likely written to a community of Christians who were experiencing some pretty serious challenges. It may be that they were caught up in the Jewish-Roman war that ended in the destruction of the Temple, or that they had recently endured persecution of one kind or another. So a big part of the purpose of Mark's Gospel—and the story of the cross in particular—is to support these Christians by letting them know that Jesus also suffered and so understands what they're going through.

That makes sense.

At the same time, Mark wants to offer Jesus as a model of being obedient even though he's afraid. In this way he encourages the people for whom he's writing his Gospel to hold on to their faith.

That's why Jesus both prays for the cup to pass but also stays faithful, saying that in the end it's not what he wants that is important, but what God wants.

Right. What else did you notice?

Well, to be honest, the disciples don't come off all that well. They totally fail Jesus during his time of need. I mean, all he asks is that they stay awake and keep him company, but they end up falling asleep—not just once but *three* different times. No wonder Jesus is upset with them.

Yeah, it's a pretty dramatic scene.

And a little heartbreaking, too, to be so let down by your friends.

So what was your impression of the disciples, on the whole, after this scene?

Not a very good one. They don't exactly come across as dependable.

And that's very much the way Mark portrays them throughout his Gospel.

Why?

I think there may be two reasons. First, this was a community of people who were struggling, perhaps suffering, and some of them may well have denied their faith under threat of persecution, or even lost their faith altogether. And it may be that some of these folks wanted to come back and rejoin the community.

So maybe Mark makes the disciples so human to emphasize that you don't have to be a hero to be a follower of Jesus. Even Christians who become afraid, who aren't dependable, and who deny their faith can still be disciples. Something like that?

I think so.

I like that. It's kind of like Mark is saying, "Look, if these guys can be Jesus' disciples, anyone can!"

NEITHER SUPERHUMAN NOR SUPERHERO

I think that's very much one of the things Mark is saying in this scene.

So what comes next?

Jesus is betrayed by Judas, one of the twelve disciples, and taken to be questioned by the religious council. At the same time, Peter follows closely behind, though he can't go inside to where Jesus is being questioned. These two mini-scenes, taken together, prove to be pretty dramatic, as Mark not only portrays Jesus as being very human, but also shows that Jesus was telling the truth.

What do you mean?

Well, it wouldn't be fair to say that Jesus was in control—that's more what we'll find in John—or that he took everything like a stoic.

Instead, what I mean is that even though Jesus was suffering greatly, it becomes more and more clear that he is who he said he was.

I'm still not following.

A little earlier in the story, at the last supper he shares with his disciples, Jesus predicts that all the disciples will desert him and that Peter—who throughout the story is clearly the chief disciple—will deny him three times. Now, at the end of the scene with the council, when the religious authorities have decided that he's guilty and begin harassing him, some yell at him, "Prophesy!" (14:65). They might have been challenging the blindfolded Jesus to tell who was hitting him, or they could have been asking him to make another bold prediction, as he had when they asked if he was the Messiah (14:62). What's interesting to me is that just at that moment Mark switches his attention to Peter. Maybe we should look at this part together:

> While Peter was below in the courtyard, one of the servant-girls of the high priest came by. When she saw Peter warming himself, she stared at him and said, "You also were with Jesus, the man from Nazareth." But he denied it, saying, "I do not know or understand what you are talking about." And he went out into the forecourt. Then the cock crowed. And the servant-girl, on seeing him, began again to say to the bystanders, "This man is one of them." But again he denied it. Then after a little while the bystanders again said to Peter, "Certainly you are one of them; for you are a Galilean." But he began to curse, and he swore an oath, "I do not know this man you are talking about." At that moment the cock crowed for the second time. Then Peter remembered that Jesus had said to him, "Before the cock crows twice, you will deny me three times." And he broke down and wept. (14:66-72)

Wow. Again, it's both dramatic and heartbreaking. But I think I see what you mean. At the same time that everyone is telling Jesus to make a prediction, one of his predictions is actually coming true. Which might be a way Mark is saying to his people that no matter how bad it looks, Jesus really was telling the truth.

Exactly.

I wonder if that's also why Mark tells us that Peter didn't just deny Jesus, but actually cursed and swore an oath. Is that possibly what some of the folks in Mark's community might have done when they were being persecuted? I mean, if they had, it would certainly be comforting to hear that Peter had done the same.

I think that's very possible and a good insight.

I also found the part about Peter weeping kind of moving, and I can see how someone who had deserted Christianity and later felt terrible about it would read that and totally be able to connect with Peter.

Right.

All right, so I think this is coming together for me. Mark wants his community to know that Jesus can understand what they're going through, that he was faithful and he encourages them to be the same, and that the disciples, including Peter, were no better than they were.

I think that's a pretty fair summary.

So where to next?

I think one more passage will be helpful. It's right near the end of the passion story, when Jesus has been crucified:

> *When it was noon, darkness came over the whole land until three in the afternoon. At three o'clock Jesus cried out with a loud voice, "Eloi, Eloi, lema sabachthani?" which means, "My God, my God, why have you forsaken me?" When some of the bystanders heard it, they said, "Listen, he is calling for Elijah." And someone ran, filled a sponge with sour wine, put it on a stick, and gave it to him to drink, saying, "Wait, let us see whether Elijah will come to take him down." Then Jesus gave a loud cry and breathed his last. And the curtain of the temple was torn in two, from top to bottom. Now when the centurion, who stood facing him, saw that in this way he breathed his last, he said, "Truly this man was God's Son!" (15:33-39)*

So what do you notice?

A couple of things, actually. First, Mark again spares no details about how difficult this is for Jesus. I mean, he cries out in what sounds like utter despair. Once again, all I can think to say is that Jesus is so very human.

Definitely, even more so when you realize that it's the only thing Jesus says on the cross in Mark.

What do you mean, it's the only thing he says in Mark? Does Jesus say other things in the other Gospels?

All total, there are seven different things Jesus says from the cross. He says three different things in Luke and three more different things in John—we'll get to those later. But in Mark and Matthew, he only says this one thing that's called the "cry of dereliction." Like you've said, Mark depicts Jesus as being very human.

I was also struck by the centurion. I mean, there he is, this Roman soldier who's just gotten done crucifying Jesus, and then he goes and says that Jesus is God's Son.

What did you make of that?

Well, it seems like if there's anyone likely to be unaffected by the cross, it would be the centurion. He's probably seen and done this before. And yet the cross gets to him, it convinces him in some way that Jesus really is God's Son.

So maybe Mark is pointing to the cross as the only place you can really see and experience God in a way that rings true, that's believable.

I like that.
There's one detail I don't understand, though, but maybe it's not that important.

Which one is that?

The part about the curtain that was torn in half. What's up with that?

That's a great question, and a little background information will help.

Okay.

The Jerusalem Temple was divided into several concentric sections. Everyone could be in the outermost areas, but as you went toward the center it become increasingly exclusive: Gentiles—people who weren't Jewish—could only go in so far. Women had to stop at a certain point. And then men. The innermost part of the Temple was called the Holy of Holies, and only the high priest could go in there and only once a year, on Yom Kippur, the Day of Atonement, in order to offer sacrifices to God.

I didn't know any of that. That's very interesting.

The Holy of Holies is the place Jews believed God's own presence was mediated to them through the high priest. And this part of the Temple was separated by a huge curtain eighty feet tall.

And it got torn when Jesus died?

That's what the Gospels tell us.

That seems like it would be pretty symbolic.

Say a little more.

Well, it sounds like this curtain that separated the presence of God from all the people was suddenly torn in half, actually torn away, making it possible for anyone to have access to God.

Or maybe signifying that you can't keep God behind a curtain, that through the cross God entered into our world and lives in a different way.

Like God has been set loose in the world. That's actually very cool. Through Jesus we are given access to God, and God has direct access to us.

That's very much a part of this Gospel's confession about Jesus.

There's one other part that I think is significant, too, although it has as much to do with the whole Gospel as it does just the passion story.

What's that?

Do you remember how we've said that no one really expected the cross?

Yeah—we said that's true in all the Gospels.

In some ways it's especially true in Mark.

What do you mean?

Remember how the disciples in Mark never get it? It's not just that they can't stay awake, but they are actually pretty clueless throughout.

How come?

I think Mark is saying that nobody would have ever, even in a million years, expected God to show up in the cross. I mean, it's not just the pain and suffering, but it's also the humiliation implied in being crucified. As we've seen, crucifixion is a pretty awful way to die. So awful, in fact, that no Roman citizen could legally be crucified. It was reserved as punishment for criminals and other non-Romans who threatened or stood up to the Roman Empire.

I guess that's why it would seem so unlikely that Jesus was really the Messiah, because you don't expect God to be working through someone who was crucified.

Exactly, and yet that's where Mark says God shows up—just where we least expect God to be.

And why does Mark say that?

Keep in mind that a lot of first-century Jewish people who were looking for the Messiah expected him to come as a political or military leader.

But what they get is Jesus, this guy who gets killed.

Right. And Mark wants to say that's not just an accident, because God *always* shows up where you least expect God to be. Instead of coming in power, God comes in weakness. Instead of coming to fight and destroy, God comes to sympathize, to suffer, and eventually to die. Instead of coming with an army, God comes in the cross.

Okay, I get the surprise element—God just doesn't do what we expect. But I'm not sure I understand why Mark wants to emphasize this point. That doesn't exactly sound like good news.

It's probably not if you're one of the powerful. You know, if you're a ruler or a warrior, you probably want a strong God, because this kind of God can protect you. But that's not Mark's community or any of the early Christians for that matter.

What do you mean?

Most of the early Christians are not from the powerful, ruling classes of either Jewish or Roman culture. Most of them are the regular working folks and poor people. Jesus' disciples, for instance, aren't businessmen or religious or political figures; they're fishermen who are pretty far down the economic ladder. There are exceptions of course—some early disciples are, in fact, wealthy and hold important positions—but they are the minority.

Interesting.

And this is particularly true of the folks Mark is writing to, who are enduring, or maybe have just come out of, a very difficult period. Whatever they once were, most of them are feeling pretty low, pretty down and out. And so Mark tells them that they don't have to be powerful to meet God; that God actually comes and meets them right where they are, in the middle of their suffering and fear and pain.

That's a powerful message. But are you saying that God only comes for powerless and poor people, and not for the rich and powerful?

I think what I'd say is that God is coming *especially* for the weak, poor, and powerless, but not *only* for them. Certainly there are moments when each one of us, no matter how strong we may feel in general, finds ourselves to be weak and vulnerable.

Like when we get sick, or when someone we love dies, or when we lose a job or suffer a miscarriage, or something like that.

Right.

Hmmm.

What?

I'm trying to think this through.

So God comes in the cross to identify with us—all of us, I suppose—but the weak and powerless, for sure, which is all of us, at some time, when we feel down and out. So Mark tells us that if we look for God to come as a strong, superhero-like warrior, we're going to be disappointed. Is that what you're saying?

Not only will we be disappointed, but we'll actually *miss* the God who comes to be with us in our suffering, to hold on to us through our suffering, to stay with us even through death to new life.

I think I see what you mean.

And what do you think?

I think it's a pretty amazing message. Like Mark is ultimately saying that God is totally, 100 percent *for* you, on your side, but that you just can't understand that apart from what Jesus does on the cross.

Right, except that it doesn't just start with the cross. Throughout Mark's Gospel, Jesus hangs out with the outcasts, the sinners, the losers, the people who have been left behind by society. In a way, his whole life and ministry bear the presence of God to those who wouldn't expect God to be with them, and all of that culminates in the cross.

Which sounds like it would be very encouraging to Mark's people who had gone through their own suffering and also to us when we feel down and out.

Exactly.

I think I like Mark's story about the cross.

I do, too.

Do you think we're ready to look at the resurrection, then?

Absolutely. Though I should warn you to be prepared to be a little freaked out.

What do you mean?

Just that Mark's version of the resurrection has been freaking people out for close to two thousand years.

49

You've got to be kidding.

Nope. Let's take a look and see. Again, pay attention to the details and let me know what you think:

> *When the sabbath was over, Mary Magdalene, and Mary the mother of James, and Salome bought spices, so that they might go and anoint him. And very early on the first day of the week, when the sun had risen, they went to the tomb. They had been saying to one another, "Who will roll away the stone for us from the entrance to the tomb?" When they looked up, they saw that the stone, which was very large, had already been rolled back. As they entered the tomb, they saw a young man, dressed in a white robe, sitting on the right side; and they were alarmed. But he said to them, "Do not be alarmed; you are looking for Jesus of Nazareth, who was cruci-fied. He has been raised; he is not here. Look, there is the place they laid him. But go, tell his disciples and Peter that he is going ahead of you to Galilee; there you will see him, just as he told you." So they went out and fled from the tomb, for terror and amazement had seized them; and they said nothing to anyone, for they were afraid. (16:1-8)*

I see what you mean by this ending freaking people out. I mean, is that really how it ends?

It sure is. What caught your attention in particular?

Two things: First, Jesus doesn't even show up in this ending. I mean, how can we call this the resurrection if the one who's supposed to be resurrected doesn't even make an appearance?

Fair enough.

And, second, the women totally fail. I mean, it's not like they've been given complicated instructions: they're told to go and tell the disciples what's just happened. You'd think they'd want to do that anyway. But they don't. They just run away, and Mark seems to go out of his way to tell us that that they don't say anything to anyone.

It sounds like this ending makes you a little uncomfortable.

More than a little! But, seriously, is this the way it really ends?

There are actually more verses in Mark's Gospel. The next ones are called the "shorter" ending of Mark, and they report that the women do eventually tell the disciples and then Jesus makes a brief appearance to send the disciples out to preach the gospel. After that comes the "longer" ending of Mark, which adds a couple of scenes that are similar to some of the resurrection accounts in the other Gospels. But most people are convinced that these were added a lot later.

Why?

Two main reasons: First, the oldest copies of Mark's Gospel don't contain these verses.

Oldest copies?

We actually don't have the original Mark (or of any of the books of the Bible, for that matter). All we have are later copies, and the oldest of these doesn't have these verses.

Second, the style and vocabulary of these two later endings doesn't match the rest of Mark's Gospel.

So you think they were added later?

Yeah, and I bet you can guess why.

It seems to me like whoever was doing the copying wanted to clean things up a bit, to make Mark sound a little more like the other Gospels, I imagine. To be honest, I can't really blame them, though I think that given what we've said so far, we should try to hear what Mark is saying rather than get freaked out by how different his version is from the others.

I agree. So if we stick with the original ending of Mark—even if it's a little unsettling—what do you make of things?

Mostly that these women completely fail. I mean, I guess they eventually had to tell someone something, or we wouldn't have Mark's Gospel at all, but in this scene they totally drop the ball.

Which doesn't seem all that unusual, does it?

Why not?
Oh, wait, I think I see. Throughout the Gospel the disciples have

regularly missed the boat—whether they're afraid, or don't understand, or whatever, they often come off as pretty clueless.

Right.

And so you're saying that maybe we shouldn't be surprised if these women also don't get it.

Right again. This could provide some relief to Mark's community if they have struggled and failed as well. Or it might be that Mark is actually trying to do just the opposite.

What do you mean?

Well, at this point in the story, absolutely no one has followed through. Nobody stayed with Jesus to the end, and now that he's been raised—according to a young man in a white robe at the tomb—no one is going to carry that story to the world.

Which makes for a pretty lousy ending, like we said.

Unless it's not the ending.

I'm not following.

There's one more person who knows that Jesus has been raised. One more person who has followed Jesus' ministry, who saw him do miracles, who heard him make predictions about his death and resurrection and about the disciples and has seen all these predictions come true.

Who's that?

You.

ME?!

You, the reader.

Oh, you mean that Mark has been telling his readers—back then, and today as well—all this stuff about Jesus so we know all that's happened.

Right. The women failed, and we're the only ones left to tell others what happened.

So maybe Mark wasn't simply trying to make the early Christians he wrote to feel better; maybe he was also saying they have another chance—another chance to go and tell, to share the news about Jesus.

Exactly. Mark creates this dramatic, open-ended story because he wants his readers—all of his readers—to pick up where the story left off, to carry the news the two messengers delivered, to continue Jesus' work.

But I'm still not sure why Jesus didn't show up. I mean, couldn't he have told the disciples all this?

Maybe. But do you think Mark's community got to see Jesus while they were suffering?

Probably not.

And what about you, when you feel down and out? Does Jesus come to give you a little one-on-one pep talk in person?

No, definitely not.

But you might have someone else tell you about Jesus, about the God who meets you in your despair and discouragement?

I see what you mean. Mark writes a story where the characters are a lot like us. They don't get a personal appearance from Jesus, and neither do we.

Right. All we have is the message. No proof. Just the promise that Jesus is raised so that we'll know not only that God meets us in our suffering, but also that God has triumphed over our suffering, even over death.

That's pretty amazing.

Yeah, I think so, too.

So Mark offers this very human Jesus who can identify with us even as he inspires us. Mark is saying that God comes to meet us, not in strength and power, but right in the middle of our suffering. That means we can only really see God in the suffering of the cross, and that because of Jesus, nothing separates us from God. Once we've heard this story, Mark wants us to go and tell others.

That's a great summary.

Thanks.

So are all the Gospel stories about the cross this packed with meaning?

Maybe we should keep reading to find out.

Sounds good. Where to next?

Let's look at Luke, who writes about ten years or so after Mark. He follows much of Mark's outline but introduces some new elements as well.

Great. Will we look at it in as much depth as we did Mark?

There's no substitute for reading the whole passion narrative, of course. But I think by focusing on a couple of details, we can appreciate how Luke builds on Mark's story to make his own distinct confession about Jesus.

So let's start back at Gethsemane, except Luke doesn't tell us that it's Gethsemane; instead, the scene is the Mount of Olives.

How come?

Luke is probably writing for a community of mostly Gentile Christians—people who weren't originally Jewish—and so he uses the better known and more general name for the area, the Mount of Olives, instead of the more specific, local name, Gethsemane.

Interesting.

Okay, like last time, just pay attention to the details:

> He came out and went, as was his custom, to the Mount of Olives; and
> the disciples followed him. When he reached the place, he said to them,
> "Pray that you may not come into the time of trial." Then he withdrew
> from them about a stone's throw, knelt down, and prayed, "Father, if you
> are willing, remove this cup from me; yet, not my will but yours be done."
> Then an angel from heaven appeared to him and gave him strength. In
> his anguish he prayed more earnestly, and his sweat became like great
> drops of blood falling down on the ground. When he got up from prayer,
> he came to the disciples and found them sleeping because of grief, and he

*said to them, "Why are you sleeping? Get up and pray that you may not
come into the time of trial."*

*While he was still speaking, suddenly a crowd came, and the one
called Judas, one of the twelve, was leading them. He approached Jesus
to kiss him; but Jesus said to him, "Judas, is it with a kiss that you are
betraying the Son of Man?" When those who were around him saw what
was coming, they asked, "Lord, should we strike with the sword?" Then
one of them struck the slave of the high priest and cut off his right ear.
But Jesus said, "No more of this!" And he touched his ear and healed him.
Then Jesus said to the chief priests, the officers of the temple police, and
the elders who had come for him, "Have you come out with swords and
clubs as if I were a bandit? When I was with you day after day in the
temple, you did not lay hands on me. But this is your hour, and the power
of darkness!" (22:39-53)*

So what struck you?

**As in Mark, Jesus is a pretty human figure, struggling to do what God wants
him to do. One difference I noticed, though, is that it seems like the disciples
come off a little better with Luke than with Mark.**

Say a little more.

**Well, in Mark the disciples fall asleep three times. But Luke only tells about
them falling asleep once. And he gives them an excuse: they fell asleep
because they were so upset.**

That's consistent with the rest of Luke's Gospel, where he regularly
offers a more sympathetic picture of the disciples than Mark does.

Why do you think he does that?

I can think of two reasons: First, keep in mind that part of the reason
Mark is so hard on the disciples is to make the point that no one is so
inadequate that they can't be a disciple. But that might not be Luke's
issue. He might want to show how the disciples were, in fact, pretty
decent people who were trying—and sometimes succeeding—to
be faithful. Second, this Gospel is just the first half of Luke's larger
work.

Really?

Yes. Luke's second book, called the Acts of the Apostles, tells the story of the early church, the time from when Jesus ascended to heaven after the resurrection to near the end of the apostle Paul's ministry. And because the main characters of this book are the disciples, I suspect Luke figured that it would be more believable if they've got their act a little more together in the Gospel. So not only does Luke tell us that they fell asleep once in this scene, but a little earlier, at the last supper, Jesus doesn't warn them about falling away, but instead promises that even though they will be tested they won't ultimately fail.

That is really a much more generous picture of the disciples.

What else did you notice?

I don't remember Jesus healing the guy whose ear got cut off in Mark.

That's right. Mark doesn't tell us about that. Throughout Luke's Gospel, Jesus is very much a compassionate healer. In fact, in his very first sermon, Jesus announces that he has come "to bring good news to the poor, proclaim release to the captives, recovery of sight to the blind, to let the oppressed go free, and to proclaim the year of the Lord's favor" (4:18-19, paraphrased).

What does that mean?

According to Luke, Jesus inaugurates a new age in the history of God's relationship with the world. In the first age, so to speak, God identified and elected Israel to be the chosen people. Through them, God would bless the world. In this second age, Jesus embodies God's love, compassion, and mercy for the world in his very person. This new age is signified by the healings and other miracles Jesus performs, and also through the declaration of God's intent to save all people. In the third age, Jesus will ascend to heaven and empower his disciples—both then and now—to carry on his work of healing and reconciliation until he comes again.

So we're living in this third age.

Right. And so we're commissioned to bear Jesus' presence in the world. That is, we're called to do the things Jesus came to do: care for the poor, release those who are captive, tend the needs of all people, and announce God's favor.

That makes what we do pretty important.

It certainly does, which is why this message of healing and reconciliation runs throughout Luke's Gospel and comes up again in the passion, particularly in this scene at the Mount of Olives, in a later scene where two political enemies—Pilate and Herod—become friends (23:12), and again at his crucifixion. So let's turn there next:

> *As they led him away, they seized a man, Simon of Cyrene, who was coming from the country, and they laid the cross on him, and made him carry it behind Jesus. A great number of the people followed him, and among them were women who were beating their breasts and wailing for him. But Jesus turned to them and said, "Daughters of Jerusalem, do not weep for me, but weep for yourselves and for your children. For the days are surely coming when they will say, 'Blessed are the barren, and the wombs that never bore, and the breasts that never nursed.' Then they will begin*

to say to the mountains, 'Fall on us'; and to the hills, 'Cover us.' For if they do this when the wood is green, what will happen when it is dry?"

Two others also, who were criminals, were led away to be put to death with him. When they came to the place that is called The Skull, they crucified Jesus there with the criminals, one on his right and one on his left. Then Jesus said, "Father, forgive them; for they do not know what they are doing." And they cast lots to divide his clothing. And the people stood by, watching; but the leaders scoffed at him, saying, "He saved others; let him save himself if he is the Messiah of God, his chosen one!" The soldiers also mocked him, coming up and offering him sour wine, and saying, "If you are the King of the Jews, save yourself!" There was also an inscription over him, "This is the King of the Jews."

One of the criminals who were hanged there kept deriding him and saying, "Are you not the Messiah? Save yourself and us!" But the other rebuked him, saying, "Do you not fear God, since you are under the same sentence of condemnation? And we indeed have been condemned justly, for we are getting what we deserve for our deeds, but this man has done nothing wrong." Then he said, "Jesus, remember me when you come into your kingdom." He replied, "Truly I tell you, today you will be with me in Paradise." (23:26-43)

Okay, so I see what you mean about Jesus being compassionate. He forgives the people who are crucifying him and is very kind to the criminal. But the whole scene somehow seems a little different.

Say a little more.

Well, it definitely shows the horror of the cross, like Mark. But, I don't know, Luke seems to do everything with a softer touch. I mean, some of the people following also seem upset. And one of the criminals is actually respectful, even comforting. So it's dark, but not quite as dark.

I think you're right. In Luke's story, people are still against him, but not everyone. As with the disciples, Luke is thinking ahead to the next part of the story, when all kinds of persons, including lots of Jews, some of whom may have been present when he died, come to believe he was the Messiah.

You said earlier that while Mark only describes Jesus as crying out in despair, Luke tells us about three things Jesus says. We just heard the first two, Jesus forgiving the crowd and promising the criminal that he'll join Jesus in paradise. What's the third?

That comes right at the end:

> It was now about noon, and darkness came over the whole land until
> three in the afternoon, while the sun's light failed; and the curtain of
> the temple was torn in two. Then Jesus, crying with a loud voice, said,
> "Father, into your hands I commend my spirit." Having said this, he
> breathed his last. When the centurion saw what had taken place, he
> praised God and said, "Certainly this man was innocent." And when all
> the crowds who had gathered there for this spectacle saw what had taken
> place, they returned home, beating their breasts. But all his acquain-
> tances, including the women who had followed him from Galilee, stood at
> a distance, watching these things. (23:44-49)

Once again, the disciples come off a little better. I mean, they may not have stayed with him, but they don't totally desert him, either, as Luke tells us that they stood at a distance, watching. But what really struck me is how much Jesus trusts God right up to the end. It's clearly agonizing and all, but he doesn't seem to despair like he does in Mark. That really comes through in the last thing he says, about putting his spirit in God's hands.

That's true. Jesus is, in every sense, righteous and trusting. That's probably why Luke reports the centurion declaring Jesus' innocence—to
show that even Gentiles can see that he is righteous.

Why is that important?

Throughout Luke's Gospel, he has stressed that Jesus really is the Jewish Messiah who has come to fulfill the promises in both the Law
and the Prophets, and save not only Israel, but all the world. So Luke
regularly shows how Jesus keeps the law at every step of his journey, and how even Romans—first Pilate (in a scene we didn't read)
and now the centurion—declare his innocence and therefore his
righteousness.

Does this follow through in the story of the resurrection, too?

59

It does. In fact, Luke adds a whole new scene.

Really?

Yeah, the first scene is similar to Mark's, except that the women do come back and tell the disciples what happened. The disciples, of course, don't believe it.

What do you mean?

Well, all the Gospels report disbelief before belief. I think they want to make the point that the news of resurrection—of life actually defeating death—really is pretty amazing and quite honestly difficult to believe. But I also think they want to tell us that maybe doubt and faith are woven together a little more closely than we might have imagined.

Can you say a little more?

Sure. We tend to think that faith is the opposite of doubt, but in the Bible faith doesn't imply that you don't have any doubt, but rather that you hang on and keep trusting God even if you do have doubts.

I think I like that. I mean, there's a whole lot I'm not sure of, and it's kind of cool to think that that's all right.
But what about this new scene?

It takes place on the evening of the first Easter, the day Jesus is raised from the dead. Two disciples are walking home, totally stunned by what happened, and Jesus joins them on the road, except they don't recognize him. So he starts to interpret the Bible and explain that all of this had to happen for God's mercy to be revealed to the whole world. Then, when he's at supper with them, he breaks the bread— tears it apart and gives it to them—and suddenly they recognize him just as he vanishes from their sight. In response, they immediately get up and go back to Jerusalem to tell the other disciples what they saw (Luke 24:13-35).

That's quite a story.

Yeah, and it again shows how Jesus fulfills the prophecy in the Jewish scriptures about being the Messiah. But it also addresses Mark's concern about how you talk about resurrection with people who have never seen Jesus in person.

I'm not sure I caught that.

That's understandable, because it's pretty subtle. But think again about what happens in Jesus' encounter with these two disciples. First, he interprets the scriptures so that they can understand them; second, he sits with them at supper and, as Luke writes, he "took bread, blessed and broke it, and gave it to them" (24:30).

That sounds kind of familiar.

It's almost identical to the way Luke describes what Jesus does at the last supper, and it's the same language that we often use in church at Holy Communion.

So first he interprets the Bible and then shares a special meal, and that's when they see him? That sounds, actually, a lot like a church service.

Exactly. It feels like Luke is saying, "If you want to see Jesus, gather with the faithful, reflect on God's Word, share the meal Jesus gives us, and through all this God will encounter you." That's ideally what the church is supposed to be.

So, like Mark, Luke wants to say something about how later Christians can also be Jesus' disciples.

Right. And, in fact, in his Acts of the Apostles, Luke goes a little further, stressing that *anyone* can be a disciple—men, women, Jews, Gentiles, slaves, free—anyone. What Jesus does through his cross and resurrection dissolves all the differences between people that we usually focus on.

That's very cool.
Since we're on the topic of Acts, though, can I ask another question?

Shoot.

If Luke wrote a second book, how does he end this part of the story about Jesus' cross and resurrection?

After this appearance to the two disciples on the road to Emmaus, Jesus appears once more to the disciples and shows them again how his life, death, and resurrection fulfill the Jewish prophecies for a Messiah and tells them that they, as his witnesses, need to share this message of God's love, healing, and forgiveness with all people. Then he tells them to wait for God to give them the power to do these things, and he ascends to heaven.

And that's where the Acts of the Apostles picks up?

In Acts, Luke recaps the Gospel for his audience and starts the story with the ascension and continues quickly to Pentecost, when the Holy Spirit comes upon the disciples and gives them the courage and ability to tell everyone about Jesus.

And this is the third age you were talking about—when Jesus' disciples share the good news about God's love and mercy and continue Jesus' work of healing and helping everyone.

Right. Jesus commissions his disciples—then and now—to be his witnesses and to do the things he's doing.

Is that kind of like Mark wanting us to pick up the message from the women when they couldn't pass it on because they were too afraid?

It's sort of like that, but in the book of Acts, Luke has the chance to go into a lot more detail about what being a follower of Jesus looks like.

So let me see if I have this straight. Luke's Jesus is also very human, but where Mark emphasized Jesus' suffering, Luke underscores a little more Jesus' tremendous compassion, healing, and trust in God. In this way, Luke shows that to be a disciple of Jesus you do the things Jesus was doing—healing, helping, and witnessing to God's love and mercy.

Right. Part of what Luke is saying is that God's power becomes evident whenever and wherever people—Jews or Gentiles—treat each other with the care and compassion that Jesus shows.

Got it.

Okay, then let's go on. Matthew next? I remember you said that was the other Gospel that relied on Mark.

Good memory. Yeah, we'll turn next to Matthew, and I think we can cover things pretty quickly, because Matthew is a whole lot like Mark, even more than Luke was. Matthew also portrays Jesus' suffering and humanity, for instance, reporting the same cry of dereliction from the cross.

So what's the major difference?

The biggest difference is that Matthew is tremendously concerned with demonstrating that Jesus is the Jewish Messiah.

Why?

By the time the evangelists—that's what the writers of Matthew, Mark, Luke, and John are sometimes called—are writing their Gospels, most of the early Christian communities are made up of both Jews and Gentiles (non-Jewish people). But it seems that Matthew's community probably has more Jewish people in it, so he's really interested in showing how Jesus fulfills Jewish prophecies about the Messiah.

We need to slow down a bit. How can Matthew's community be both Christian and Jewish?

That's a great question. It's easy for us to forget that in the early decades of Christianity, a person's identity as "Christian" as opposed to "Jewish" wasn't nearly as distinct as ours is today. Jesus is Jewish, and all of his disciples are as well, as were the first folks who believed in Jesus because of the witness of the disciples.

Okay, I think I'm following.

That changes when the apostle Paul comes on the scene and takes the gospel to Gentiles. And it's not very long before there are all kinds of Christians—Jews, Greeks, Romans, and so forth. But early on, folks probably didn't think of themselves so much as Christian—something that is different from Jewish—but instead as Jews who believed that Jesus was the Jewish Messiah.

And Matthew's community is one of these groups?

Most likely. Again, we don't know for sure, but from the number of times Matthew quotes Jewish scripture—what Christians call the Old Testament—it sure sounds like Matthew is talking with people who know the Jewish traditions.

And so he wants to assure them that Jesus really is the Jewish Messiah?

Right. And he does this especially in two ways. One, he regularly interprets Jesus' ministry in terms of the life of Moses. So when Jesus preaches his most famous sermon, he preaches from a mountain.

That's the Sermon on the Mount?

Right. Luke, on the other hand, describes Jesus as preaching that sermon on an open plain. But Matthew describes Jesus on a mountain, because that reminds you of Moses. Similarly, Matthew breaks up Jesus' teaching into five parts, which would remind people of the five books of the Law (Genesis through Deuteronomy), which tradition said were written by Moses.

Okay, that makes sense.

The second thing Matthew does is to point out how what happens to Jesus falls in line with the Jewish prophecies about the Messiah, and that shows up especially in his story of the events leading up to the cross. For instance, let's look at the scene in Gethsemane when Jesus is betrayed:

> *While he was still speaking, Judas, one of the twelve, arrived; with him was a large crowd with swords and clubs, from the chief priests and the elders of the people. Now the betrayer had given them a sign, saying, "The one I will kiss is the man; arrest him." At once he came up to Jesus and said, "Greetings, Rabbi!" and kissed him. Jesus said to him, "Friend, do what you are here to do." Then they came and laid hands on Jesus and arrested him. Suddenly, one of those with Jesus put his hand on his sword, drew it, and struck the slave of the high priest, cutting off his ear. Then Jesus said to him, "Put your sword back into its place; for all who take the sword will perish by the sword. Do you think that I cannot appeal to my Father, and he will at once send me more than twelve legions of angels? But how then would the scriptures be fulfilled, which say it must happen*

in this way?" At that hour Jesus said to the crowds, "Have you come out
with swords and clubs to arrest me as though I were a bandit? Day after
day I sat in the temple teaching, and you did not arrest me. But all this
has taken place, so that the scriptures of the prophets may be fulfilled."
Then all the disciples deserted him and fled. (26:47-56)

I think I see what you mean—twice Jesus goes out of his way to say that what's
happening is to fulfill the scriptures.

Right, and beyond that, there are all kinds of other references to the
Old Testament, from Pilate's "washing his hands" of Jesus' death—a
reference to a passage in Deuteronomy—to several references to the
Psalms. All of this is to make the case for a Jewish audience that Jesus
really does fulfill the prophecies about the Jewish Messiah.

Interesting.

Yeah, it is, although there's a dark side to this as well.

What do you mean?

It's very likely that when Matthew is writing there is some controversy among the Jewish community about Jesus—whether or not he was really the Messiah—and that people are beginning to take sides. So Matthew doesn't just present his evidence and hope people believe in Jesus; he goes out of his way to paint his rivals in a bad light.

I'm not sure I'm following.

The major religious figures of Judaism after the fall of the Jerusalem Temple are the Pharisees, the leaders of the local synagogues. They don't believe that Jesus is the Messiah, and so the people in Matthew's community have at least two options: side with Matthew in believing Jesus is the Messiah or side with the Pharisees. So it often feels like Matthew's Gospel is, in part, a running argument with the Pharisees about who's interpreting the Jewish scriptures and traditions correctly.

Can you give an example?

Sure. Not only does Matthew make the references to the Old Testament that we were talking about, but he also goes out of his way to show that Jesus' death was the fault of the Jewish religious authorities. Let's look at this troubling scene with Pontius Pilate, the Roman governor:

> Now at the festival the governor was accustomed to release a prisoner for the crowd, anyone whom they wanted. At that time they had a notorious prisoner, called Jesus Barabbas. So after they had gathered, Pilate said to them, "Whom do you want me to release for you, Jesus Barabbas or Jesus who is called the Messiah?" For he realized that it was out of jealousy that they had handed him over. While he was sitting on the judgment seat, his wife sent word to him, "Have nothing to do with that innocent man, for today I have suffered a great deal because of a dream about him." Now the chief priests and the elders persuaded the crowds to ask for Barabbas and to have Jesus killed. The governor again said to them, "Which of the two do you want me to release for you?" And they said, "Barabbas." Pilate said to them, "Then what should I do with Jesus who is called the Messiah?" All of them said, "Let him be crucified!" Then he asked, "Why, what evil has he done?" But they shouted all the more, "Let him be crucified!"

> *So when Pilate saw that he could do nothing, but rather that a riot was beginning, he took some water and washed his hands before the crowd, saying, "I am innocent of this man's blood; see to it yourselves." Then the people as a whole answered, "His blood be on us and on our children!" So he released Barabbas for them; and after flogging Jesus, he handed him over to be crucified (27:15-26).*

Oh my goodness—I see what you mean. It's like Matthew wants to make sure we realize this isn't Pilate's fault, but instead that the Jewish religious leaders are totally to blame.

Exactly. In the beginning of Matthew's Gospel, when Herod and the chief priests want to kill Jesus, the magi (or wisemen)—who aren't Jewish—are warned in a dream not to tell Herod where the baby Jesus is. Now another Gentile, Pilate's wife, has a dream warning her not to cooperate with the chief priests and Jewish elders.

Right, and then Pilate says he wants nothing to do with punishing Jesus. Is this only in Matthew, or do Mark and Luke describe it this way, too?

Mark and Luke both tell about the request to free Barabbas, but no one else says that Pilate washed his hands of Jesus' death or, worse, that the crowds cry that they accept full responsibility for everything.

Yeah, I was really struck by the cry of the crowds, "His blood be on us and our children." It just sounds so harsh.

It is. And while we can maybe understand how Matthew wrote something like that when his community was in the minority and having a bitter rivalry with their Jewish neighbors, through the centuries it's done tremendous damage. In some time periods, Christians used this blood oath as an excuse to beat up Jewish people during Holy Week.

So how do we deal with this element of Matthew's Gospel today?

Well, when you read Matthew—and John, too, as we'll see—you need to sometimes explain to others the original setting of the Gospels, and how the community Matthew addressed was likely in the minority and feeling pressured. But eventually Christians became the majority and held the power in Western society. That's been true for much of the last fifteen hundred years. We have to be cautious not to let Matthew's accusing tone guide our words and actions. During Hitler's reign, for instance, Christians would use this passage to justify imprisoning and killing Jews.

That's awful.

Yes, it is. Scripture is powerful, and Christians have used it for good and evil over the centuries. That's why it's important for today's Christians to read Matthew alongside the other Gospels.

I'm not sure what you mean.

Mark and Luke, for instance, not only do not let Pilate off the hook, but they also show that there were clear political dimensions to Jesus' ministry, so it's not surprising that it's the Romans who actually crucify Jesus as a political prisoner. I think recognizing these two things will go a long way to helping us read the Gospels better.

Okay, thanks; that's helpful. I can see how it's important that today's Christians not only point out why Matthew is writing the way he did but also point to the larger picture of Jesus in order to stand against prejudice.

That's exactly right.

And what about Matthew's story of the resurrection?

That won't take long, because Matthew again follows Mark's outline. But Matthew's story is far more dramatic, with an earthquake and flashing angel; a cover-up story involving the chief priests—part of the ongoing rivalry we talked about; and an appearance from Jesus where he commissions the disciples to take the gospel into all the world.

Got it. So, let's see if I can summarize. We've got Mark and Matthew, pretty similar in terms of wanting us to realize how human Jesus was and how very real his suffering was, though Mark leaves things open-ended and Matthew ties things up so that we'll know the God who acted in the Old Testament is again at work, this time through Jesus. And then there's Luke, who's more interested in how Jesus demonstrates God's love, compassion, and healing. Is that right?

Again, I'd say that's a very good summary.

Thanks. So, I guess we're on to John next. And you said this one was pretty different.

Very different. Let's go back to Gethsemane, except that John doesn't call it Gethsemane, or the Mount of Olives, but instead describes it as a garden.

I thought it was always called the Garden of Gethsemane.

We *do* usually call it that. But we get Gethsemane from Mark and Matthew; only John calls it a garden.

How come?

Let's follow along and see:

> *After Jesus had spoken these words, he went out with his disciples across the Kidron valley to a place where there was a garden, which he and his disciples entered. Now Judas, who betrayed him, also knew the place, because Jesus often met there with his disciples. So Judas brought a detachment of soldiers together with police from the chief priests and the Pharisees, and they came there with lanterns and torches and weapons. Then Jesus, knowing all that was to happen to him, came forward and asked them, "Whom are you looking for?" They answered, "Jesus of Nazareth." Jesus replied, "I am he." Judas, who betrayed him, was standing with them. When Jesus said to them, "I am he," they stepped back and fell to the ground. Again he asked them, "Whom are you looking for?" And they said, "Jesus of Nazareth." Jesus answered, "I told you that I am he. So if you are looking for me, let these men go." This was to fulfill the word that he had spoken, "I did not lose a single one of those whom you gave me." Then Simon Peter, who had a sword, drew it, struck the high priest's slave, and cut off his right ear. The slave's name was Malchus. Jesus said to Peter, "Put your sword back into its sheath. Am I not to drink the cup that the Father has given me?" (18:1-11)*

I see what you mean. This almost seems like a totally different story. Well, maybe not *totally* different; the basic outline is the same, but it has a completely different feel.

Say a little more.

Well, for one thing, there's no prayer that this won't happen. No "If it's possible, remove this cup." In fact, near the end he says almost the exact opposite. After Peter takes out his sword, Jesus says, "Am I not to drink the cup the Father has given me?" It's like he wants everything to happen, or at least he is totally ready for it.

> I think you're right. Jesus, according to John, is completely prepared for what is about to happen. In fact, he came into the world for this one purpose. Earlier he says that he is the Good Shepherd who lays down his life for the sheep, and then he goes on to say, "No one takes it from me, but I lay it down of my own accord. I have power to lay it down, and I have power to take it up again" (10:18).

So in this story, Jesus is pretty much in complete control.

> Yes. That's, in part, why Jesus goes to this garden. He knows that Judas knows where it is.

Yeah, you had mentioned that John is the only one who calls it a garden. What's up with that?

> John, like Matthew, has a strong sense of how Jesus' life and death fulfill Jewish prophecy. And John, again like Matthew, not only shows this by citing particular passages, but also by making theological references. In the beginning of John's Gospel, for instance, he starts out by saying, "In the beginning was the Word . . ." (1:1), and almost anyone familiar with Jewish scriptures would hear in John's "In the beginning" echoes of how the whole biblical story starts in Genesis: "In the beginning when God created . . ." (Genesis1:1).
>
> So here, when someone hears *garden*, they might very well go back to the story of the Garden of Eden, where God created humans and where humans fell into temptation.

But in this garden Jesus isn't tempted; in fact, it's the exact opposite—he's completely faithful.

> Right. And so in a sense he succeeds where Adam and Eve failed. Not only that, but he also demonstrates the power he has and chooses not to use.

How so?

Did you notice that when Jesus asks who they're looking for and answers that it is he (Jesus of Nazareth), John writes that the soldiers Judas brought stepped back and fell to the ground?

Yeah, I wondered about that.

Well, a couple of details help to get at the more dramatic nature of John's portrayal: First, what Jesus says isn't really "I am he" but just "I am," which is the name God revealed to Moses at the burning bush (Exodus 3). We fill in the implied "he" to make it sound better, but it really is Jesus claiming the divine name, "I AM."

And that's why they fall to the ground?

Right—all six hundred of them.

What?

Well, it reads that Judas brought a detachment, or cohort, of Roman soldiers, and that's about six hundred men.

Why in the world would Judas need so many men?

He doesn't. But this is part of John's point. Jesus is *that* powerful. Judas brings six hundred men, and yet they are all thrown off their feet when Jesus claims his divine identity. So there's no question about who's in control here, or that Jesus goes to the cross of his own accord.

And John's whole story about the cross is like this? Jesus being totally in command of things?

Pretty much. It comes through in a lot of little details. For instance, Mark, Luke, and Matthew all tell that a man, Simon of Cyrene, was pulled from the crowd to help Jesus carry his cross—which makes sense, since Jesus had already been whipped and beaten and must have been exhausted. But John goes out of his way to say that Jesus carried his cross by himself (19:18). And then, at the cross, Jesus says a couple of things that are different from the other accounts.

That's right. Mark and Matthew have Jesus saying the same single thing—his cry of abandonment—and Luke reports Jesus' saying three things, each of which show him to be compassionate, forgiving, and trusting to the end. So what about John?

In John, Jesus says three things also, and we can look at them together. As usual, pay attention to what you notice:

> Meanwhile, standing near the cross of Jesus were his mother, and his mother's sister, Mary the wife of Clopas, and Mary Magdalene. When Jesus saw his mother and the disciple whom he loved standing beside her, he said to his mother, "Woman, here is your son." Then he said to the disciple, "Here is your mother." And from that hour the disciple took her into his own home.
>
> After this, when Jesus knew that all was now finished, he said (in order to fulfill the scripture), "I am thirsty." A jar full of sour wine was standing there. So they put a sponge full of the wine on a branch of hyssop and held it to his mouth. When Jesus had received the wine, he said, "It is finished." Then he bowed his head and gave up his spirit. (19:25-30)

Okay, so the first thing that sticks out is that not all the disciples run away.

That's right, three women remain, as well as a disciple that goes unnamed in John's Gospel but is regularly referred to as "the disciple Jesus loved."

And he tells them to take care of each other?

Yes, although it might be a little more than that. He actually tells them to become son and mother to each other. So, in a sense, Jesus is creating a new family, a Christian family in which people are related to each other not because of your blood ties but because they are disciples.

And he does all this while hanging from the cross?

Keep in mind that this is part of John's theology. The cross isn't a defeat for Jesus. In fact, it's the opposite; it's the place where God's glory is most fully revealed. Throughout John's Gospel, Jesus will refer to his "hour" and the time of his "glory," and both of those are now, at the cross.

What else struck you?

Well, he says that he's thirsty, which might make you think that, as with Mark and Matthew, John is showing Jesus' human side, that he has needs like the rest of us. But it almost sounds like he does this to fulfill scripture, not because he's really all that thirsty.

I think you're right. Further, the hyssop branch that they put the sponge on would, frankly, never have held a sponge.

What do you mean?

Hyssop is more of a plant than a tree; actually, it's something of an herb that had some medicinal value. It is primarily known from the Exodus story, where the Israelites are commanded to "dip it in the blood that is in the basin, and touch the lintel and the two doorposts with the blood in the basin" (Exodus12:22). This becomes part of the Passover story. So at the cross it would kind of be like trying to put a sponge of wine onto the end of a palm branch.

So why does John describe it this way?

One of the big points that John wants to make is that Jesus is the new Passover Lamb. John the Baptist describes him that way in the beginning of John's Gospel. There's all kinds of symbolism to that effect as in this scene, and Jesus' death actually occurs at the same time the Passover lambs would have been slaughtered.

And that's different than Matthew, Mark, and Luke?

It is. In all four accounts, Jesus dies on a Friday. In Matthew, Mark, and Luke, that day is Passover. Passover, though, like Christmas, can fall on any day of the week. It happens to be on a Friday in these three Gospels. In John, though, Passover falls on a Saturday, and the Friday on which Jesus dies is the day before, called the Day of Preparation, when everything was prepared for the Passover celebration, including slaughtering the Passover lambs.

That's fascinating. John wants to make a point about who Jesus is, but he's not so concerned about whether he is historically accurate.

That's well put.

So the third and final thing Jesus says is, "It is finished." After everything else in John's Gospel, I have a hard time believing he was saying, "I'm so glad that's over."

No, you're absolutely right. Here, "finished" has more of the sense of an accomplishment, like the feeling of achieving what he's set out to do.

Like "mission accomplished"?

Exactly.

So, all of this is really interesting. But it also makes me wonder why John offers such a different picture of Jesus than the others.

And, again, I think the answer is partly dependent on who we think are John's readers. Some experts believe he is addressing a community of Jewish Christians who until relatively recently had been worshiping in the local synagogues. But they may have found themselves at odds with their fellow Jews or may have been expelled from the synagogue because they believed that Jesus was the Jewish Messiah.

In a way, John's community is similar to those of Mark and Matthew. Like Mark's, John's community has been going through some stressful times—perhaps not persecution, but experiencing a sense of being cut off from its spiritual community. And, like Matthew, John is trying to reassure his community that Jesus really is the Jewish Messiah, and that the community is being faithful to its Jewish heritage in claiming Jesus as the Messiah.

I can see John's similarity to Matthew, in terms of showing how what happens to Jesus fulfills scripture, but the tie to Mark is harder to see. Mark's Jesus is so incredibly human and, like we said, he seems to be confessing that God shows up in weakness rather than strength. John, though, seems to be saying almost the opposite.

You're absolutely right. What I meant is that Mark and John offer two contrasting answers to a similar question. If Mark's community is suffering, he's saying that God meets them in their suffering. John, however, is encouraging his community to persevere amid suffering, trusting that, because God is strong enough to raise Jesus from the dead, God will also bring them through their difficulties as well.

And I can see how, depending on your circumstances, each of these "answers" could be helpful. I mean, there might be times when knowing God sympathizes with you is incredibly valuable, and others when it's important to have a sense that God can pull you out of your difficulty.

I think you're right.

So what about John's story of the resurrection? Does that have a similar emphasis on Jesus' power and strength?

John, perhaps not surprisingly, also has a different account of the resurrection than the other three Gospels, though it still follows the basic outline. While it's definitely worth reading on its own, I don't think we need to go into much detail here.

So that's it, then. Four accounts of Jesus' death and resurrection, all offering different details and perspectives.

And all contributing to how Christians over the centuries have tried to make sense of the cross.

That's what I was going to ask, actually.

What?

Well, given these different portraits, how have Christians made sense of them all? I appreciate that they decided four distinct portraits would be better than one seamless one, but how did they end up working with these four to say something really clear about the cross?

That's a great question, and while there have been many, many different interpretations of the cross—which maybe isn't surprising given the different Gospel pictures we've been talking about—we can group most of them into three schools of thought. Each looks at the cross in a distinct way.

Three, not four, to match the four Gospels?

No; although I can see why you'd guess that. Each Gospel gives us a distinct description of the passion narrative and its meaning. Later theologians read the Gospels together and try to offer interpretations that are based on the combined stories and meanings of all four, not just of one Gospel at a time. They might, as we will discover, emphasize one part of the Gospel stories or focus on one theme more than others, but they're essentially trying to deal with all of them. So we've ended up with the three schools, or three theories, of atonement that I mentioned.

I think that's probably the place to turn next.

Then let's do it.

Insights and Questions

CHAPTER 3

Ransom and Victory

I'm intrigued by something you just said.

What's that?

You talked about the difference between how the Gospels *describe* the passion of Jesus and how later theologians *interpret* it. Can you say a little more?

Sure. The four Gospels are all stories—accounts of the life, death, and resurrection of Jesus. They were written to help order and make sense of all the various stories of Jesus that were floating around at the time. The writers wanted to help people to believe that Jesus is the Messiah and also to understand what their belief means for their lives given their immediate challenges and concerns. As a big part of that, they describe the events leading to Jesus' arrest and crucifixion and the report of his resurrection. They aren't just descriptions, of course; they are themselves interpretations, as each of them tells the story in a particular way to make a particular point and speak to the concerns of a particular community.

We said they offered different portraits to voice different perspectives, or confessions, of what Jesus' death and resurrection mean.

Right. But those interpretations are lodged in the descriptions themselves. Whatever else the Gospels are or do, they remain stories about Jesus. In other words, none of the Gospels narrates part of Jesus' life and then stops and has the author interpret it: "Now, the reason Jesus told the parable of the prodigal son is so that we would understand that God is like a patient parent, always willing to wait for wayward children to return."

That would kind of ruin the story, I suspect. Like when you have to explain the punch line of a joke.

Exactly. Stories are effective precisely because they *don't* tell you everything. They give enough details for you to follow the narrative trail the author has set, but also leave enough gaps that require you to fill them in with your imagination and figure some things out for yourself. We care about stories because we enter into them imaginatively and make them our own.

I wonder if that's why whenever a favorite book is made into a movie, the movie never quite seems to do the book justice.

I think you're probably right. You've filled in the gaps differently than the screenwriters, actors, and director.

So when *Harry Potter* was made into a movie, for instance, I remember thinking that they got Ron just right, but I didn't imagine Hermione to look that way at all.

I had the same reaction.

It's not that their vision is wrong. In fact, I love the way Emma Watson has brought Hermione to life. It's just not what I'd imagined while reading the book.

I know what you mean. A good book not only gets you to fill in the gaps with your imagination, but also gets you invested in the way you've imagined something. Ultimately, I think it's a mark of just how effective J. K. Rowling, or any author for that matter, is at engaging your imagination in the first place.

And we saw that in the Gospels, too, that they told some details but left others for us to fill in, figure out, or wonder about.

That's right. So while the Gospels describe the cross—and while those descriptions certainly offer confessions about what the cross means—those confessions are *implicit*, or contained within the context of each story. Later theologians interpret the stories and make new confessions. They try to explain, make *explicit*, the meaning of the cross outside the context of the Gospel stories.

But can you do that? I mean, can you ever really explain a good story without somehow ruining it?

That's a great question, one we may want to return to from time to time. For now, I think it's probably safe to say that you can't ever fully explain any great story. Ultimately, stories are something to be experienced more than explained. But I also think it makes sense to want to explain some details about them. That's what the study of literature is, in many ways, as well as all the discussion boards and fan blogs we have today about great books and movies—attempts to get beneath the story so that we can understand and enjoy the story even more.

And that's what theologians try to do with the stories of the cross?

Right. They want to get underneath them and explain them. Because they believe the Bible is not just another story, but *the* Story that tells us most truly who we are and what purpose our lives may have, theologians want to open it up and explain the story enough so that we can enter into it and thereby encounter God. And because the cross stands at the center of this story, they give particular attention to helping us understand it.

That's challenging enough with a single story. Doesn't having four Gospels complicate things a little?

Actually, it complicates things a lot. And don't forget about the rest of the New Testament. The apostle Paul, for instance, had a lot to say about the cross. And several of the other New Testament letters are important, too.

I had forgotten about that. That means there are a lot of details and ideas about the cross to keep in mind.

That's probably why there have been so many different attempts to make sense of the cross over the centuries. That's also why we'll need to pay attention to the choices different theologians make.

What do you mean?

Remember our discussion of the different Gospel stories of the passion? The Gospel writers focused on different details to tell their stories. When you have four different accounts, there are enough different distinct details that no one theory can explain them all. So, the theologians had to make choices, emphasizing some details while leaving out others. At the same time, the theologians tended to draw on imagery from their own time and place to create their theories. And they responded to the questions they and their contemporaries had.

Like the Gospel writers themselves did?

Very much so. And, to tell you the truth, like we do.

How so?

Well, we also are not only interested in what happened with Mark's community that shaped that Gospel but are also interested in how his Gospel speaks to us today. And that's what these theologians were doing, too, even if they didn't always realize it: they were interpreting the biblical witness in light of their questions and circumstances so that the message of the cross would speak to their own time and people.

But if we have all these different interpretations, how can you tell which theory is right—or at least the best one?

Well, if you get into a discussion with a friend about the meaning of the sacrifice Harry Potter's mother made for him—and you each propose an explanation, how do you finally decide which one is right?

Well, first you look at the story. You see if the idea or theory explains the important details.

Right; and it will be important for us to do that with these theories as well.

But like we just said, with so many details no one theory can explain them all.

Is that really all that different than when dealing with a book like *Harry Potter*? After all, even though there is a single author, there are seven books in that series and countless references to his mom's sacrifice. And then there are the movies, which are also interpretations of the books and involve screenwriters, directors, actors, and the rest. We also probably have those in mind when we're talking about the meaning of his mom's sacrifice.

I see what you mean. Details alone don't do it. I guess you end up going with the explanation that *feels* right to you.

Can you say a little more about that?

You know, I'm not sure I can. I mean, it's hard to explain. Sometimes one explanation just seems more right to you. You might not even agree with the people you're talking with, and you finally can't prove your point, but I guess the explanation you go with is the one that explains things best for you, the one that helps you understand the story best.

I know what you mean, and that's going to be very true with the theories about the cross we're going to discuss, too, which will be good to remember.

What do you mean?

Some Christians have tended to make the way they understand the cross the absolute and only way any good Christian can understand the cross. And I think that's a mistake.

Why?

Because, as we just said, the best stories are those that can only be *experienced*. They can't be fully explained. Various interpretations of the cross are helpful, but no single one of them fully exhausts the potential for the passion narratives to have an effect on people, to move them to faith in the God made known through Jesus.

So when you choose only one and say all the rest are wrong, then you're limiting the power of the Gospel stories to represent God in the fullest way possible and in this way really affect people.

Exactly. As we saw with the Gospels, you might find one way of understanding the cross particularly helpful at one time in your life or during one set of circumstances, but at another time, or while facing other challenges, you might find another way of understanding the cross helpful.

I think I see what you mean. But does that mean *any* explanation about the cross is valid?

No. There have been lots of different interpretations of the cross over the centuries, and some have definitely been better than others.

How do you decide which ones are better?

Well, Christians have determined which explanations are worth hanging on to by first asking how well any interpretation makes sense of the various details about the cross in the Gospel stories. And second, Christians look at how well an interpretation makes sense of our life in the world. We'll look at three main ways Christians have interpreted the cross. In my opinion, none of them is the only way to understand the cross, and we'll want to ask critical questions about each one. Nevertheless, each view has proved very helpful to Christians at different times and may still be helpful to us today depending on our circumstances.

You mentioned that some time ago, that there are several . . . What did you call them?

Theories of atonement?

Yeah, that was it.

You could also call them models, systems, or even points of view. I chose "theories" because it reminds us that the theologians proposing them really were trying to figure things out and make sense of the cross.

Got it. But what about "atonement"? Could you say a little more about what that means?

Sure. Atonement actually means just what it says: it's concerned with the question of how you repair or restore something that is broken.

So, quite literally, it means to be "at one" or "in accord" with some-one, or "at-one-ment." So when you make atonement for something, you are doing something to repair a broken relationship.

And that's the question with the cross—how Jesus' death repairs our broken relationship with God?

That's right. Which gives us some clues about what to pay attention to.

What do you mean?

If you're going to fix something, you need to know what's broken, what the problem is. So each theory of atonement will have some-thing to say about what's gone wrong, what the human problem or predicament is. And, of course, we'll also want to know what's needed to fix it, what's necessary to restore things. In this case, that's asking about Jesus—why his cross was necessary and how it achieved atonement.

So one of the things we'll look for in thinking through these theories is their understanding of what's gone wrong, and a second is how to fix it.

Right. And because atonement is about restoring a relationship, we'll also want to see what each theory of atonement says about the two participants in the relationship—God and humanity. We'll discover a lot about what the theory says about us when we talk about what's broken, but we'll also want to pay close attention to what each theory, or model, says about who God is, about what kind of God is at work in and through the cross.

Okay. So we'll ask what each theory says about God. That makes three things to pay attention to. Is there anything else?

The last thing will be to ask what picture or understanding of the Christian life each theory gives.

I'm not sure I understand.

Once you have a sense of what's gone wrong and what is needed to fix it, then you should also have a pretty good idea of the kind of life that will support the new, repaired relationship. That is, if we were talking about an everyday relationship like the kind we have with friends, we might diagnose the problem as poor communication and then recommend that these friends set aside time to talk to each other. Or maybe the problem is that each of them is holding on to some resentment about what the other did a long time ago, and so you not only need to get those issues on the table and deal with them, you also need to commit to talking about things that bother you in the future so that you don't allow resentment to build up again.

I think I see what you mean.

When it comes to Christian faith, the questions become: What kind of life do Christians lead in light of the problems they identified and the solutions proposed? What picture of our life in faith with God and with each other does each model propose?

Okay, I think I've got it. We're going to pay attention to four things as we think through each theory of atonement and try to make sense of the cross. Each is essentially trying to answer a question:

What is God like?

What's broken about the relationship between God and humanity?

ATONEMENT

How does Jesus' cross repair what's broken?

What picture of the Christian life is given?

- **What's broken about the relationship between God and humanity?**
- **How does Jesus' cross repair what's broken?**
  How, that is, does atonement happen?
- **What is God like?**
- **What picture of the Christian life does each theory give?**

That's exactly right.

So, do you think you're ready to jump in?

Absolutely. Where do we start?

As I mentioned, there have been a number of explanations of the cross over the years—too many to cover all of them in detail. Of them all, though, three have stood out as the most important and most widely accepted. One described the cross as ransom and victory; another as substitution, satisfaction, and sacrifice; and another as example and encouragement. When we looked at the Gospels, we started with the earliest Gospel, Mark, and I think it might make similar sense to start with the earliest theory of atonement. Like the Gospels, these theories each developed over time as well.

Okay, so is the earliest theory of atonement the cross as ransom and victory?

Yes, it is, and this theory was popular among Christians for almost a thousand years. I should warn you, though, that of all three, it will probably feel the most peculiar.

Really, why?

Mostly because our view of the world has changed dramatically over the years, and this understanding of the cross is strongly influenced by views and assumptions of the ancient world, some of which will feel very foreign to us. So perhaps it will be most helpful to first describe it in general and then to go about asking and answering our four questions to help us assess it.

Sounds good.

Okay, so the ancient theory of atonement, sometimes called the classical theory—because it comes from the classical, Greco-Roman world—understands world history as the dramatic struggle between good and evil. In Christian terms, that gets played out more specifically as the struggle between God and the devil (who is also sometimes called Satan). The first move in this drama is God's creation of the world where everything is, as God pronounced, "good." The second is when the devil, in the form of a serpent, tempts Adam and Eve to eat the forbidden fruit, and they succumb to that temptation and are banished from the Garden of Eden. Traditionally that scene is called "the fall," referring to Adam and Eve's fall from a state of grace—being in right relationship with God—to being in a state of sin—alienated from God because of their disobedience.

Okay, I think I'm with you so far.

So at this point in the drama, Satan holds the upper hand. In fact, from here on out, Satan holds the upper hand.

Why?

Early Christians believed that this original sin of Adam and Eve taints, or stains, all of humanity. That means that the whole human race lives in this state of sin, this state of disobedience, which in turn means that the devil has a claim on us.

A claim? I'm not sure I understand.

Again, it's a little tricky because we don't often think this way. But alongside the biblical story of Adam and Eve, there are other stories early Christians know about the fall of the devil.

Okay, now I *know* I'm not following.

In some teachings in both Judaism and early Christianity of this time, there are stories that the devil was once an angel; in fact, one of the most powerful of God's angels. But this angel, sometimes named Lucifer, rebelled against God and led other angels into rebellion also. Ever since then, the devil is given charge over all those who rebel.

You're right. This is pretty different from the way we often think.

Maybe it will help to look at it this way. According to the ancient world, there were only two choices you can make or, better, only two sides or teams you can be a part of. You can either be part of God's team—which means obeying God—or be part of the devil's team—which is for all those who disobey God.

Ah, I think I see. So because Adam and Eve disobey God, they're on the devil's team.

Right, and it doesn't really matter if they choose this team willingly, or were tricked by the devil into sinning and so assigned to it, or just happened to make a naive choice and fell onto it. No matter how it happened, Adam and Eve fell from grace and are now on the devil's side of things.

Got it. So that's why the devil has a claim on Adam and Eve.

Right; in this life and for all eternity.

But what does that have to do with us? Why does Adam and Eve's disobedience affect all humanity?

Good question, and complicated, too. See, Adam and Eve not only fall from grace into a state of sin, but when they do so, all of their offspring—and all generations ever since—are born into this state of sin, this condition where it's easier to disobey rather than obey God.

So we're being punished for Adam and Eve's mistake? That doesn't seem fair.

Not exactly. At the heart of this story, which is meant to be more descriptive than explanatory, is the belief that we inherit Adam and Eve's weakness, their predisposition to take the easy road and disobey God, to look out for ourselves rather than to put others first, and to make bad choices out of our own insecurity and ignorance. But, the thing is, we make that condition our own all the time.

What do you mean?

Just that whatever predisposition to sin we may have, sooner or later we live into it by actually sinning. Ultimately, it's not Adam and Eve's sin that matters to us but our own sin—meaning that each one of us puts himself or herself first, or hurts others, or doesn't care for creation, or in so many other ways disobeys God.

Okay, I think I've got it. Adam and Eve may set the example, but we follow it all too easily, and this puts us on the devil's team, so to speak, and gives the devil claim over us.

Exactly. And the consequence of this disobedience is separation from God in death. Because we sin, we cannot enjoy eternal life with God.

So this is the dilemma the early Christians wrestle with? Or, to put it in the terms we talked about earlier, this is what's broken. Because of Adam and Eve's disobedience, and because of the disobedience of every human since Adam and Eve, the devil and death have a claim on us.

Right.

And so this is what the cross is supposed to fix.

Right again.

And how does the cross do that? How does it address this problem?

This is where things get interesting.

Oh great, because up 'till now everything has been so run of the mill!

I know what you mean, but bear with me. This way of putting things together really does get kind of intriguing.

So like we said, here's the problem: the devil has claim to every human being because of sin, and that means that every single one of us—no one excepted—is going to miss out on eternal life with God. Death will separate us from God forever.

Interestingly, many early Christians think of this whole thing almost as a contract. God set up the rules early on—those who obey belong to God; those who disobey belong to Satan. And so when we disobey, we naturally belong to the devil; those are the rules. But the problem is that God still loves humanity and wants, somehow, to win us back.

And so it sounds like the real problem is not just how God is going to win us back but also how God is going to abide by the rules God set up.

That's exactly it.

And that's where Jesus comes into the picture?

Yes, that's where Jesus comes in, and he enters the picture as the one who is *both* human and God.

Okay, we'll need to slow down a bit.

No problem.

One of the early Christian beliefs that is still at the heart of the Christian faith is that, in Jesus, God became human.

We talked a bit about that before, how what you see in God is what you get. Though I can't remember what that's called.

Incarnation—Latin for "in the flesh." And you're right—it's the belief that in Jesus we get the essential God. That's because, according to Christian faith, the immortal and all-powerful God took on mortal flesh and became human, experiencing all the ups and downs, possibilities and limitations of human life. John's Gospel sums it up by saying that the eternal Word "became flesh and lived among us" (1:14); that is, God became human in Jesus.

I think I'm following, though I can't say I understand it.

You're not alone. It took the early church three or four centuries to figure it out. Maybe what's most important to keep in mind at this point is the confession that somehow, in Jesus, God is both fully God and at the same time fully human just like us.

Okay, I can live with that for now. But how does this deal with the problem of the devil having claim over all humanity?

There are essentially three parts to this.

Part one: because Jesus is human, the devil assumes he has a claim on Jesus and so has a right to oversee Jesus' death.

Part two: because Jesus is God—and therefore sinless; that is, he hasn't done anything wrong and so hasn't been put on the devil's team—the devil actually doesn't have a claim on Jesus.

Part three: that means that when the devil claims Jesus on the cross, the devil actually overextends his reach and loses his claim not only on Jesus but also on all humanity.

Wait, wait, wait. I'm totally lost.

Like I said, it's complicated.

Actually, I think you said *interesting*.

Complicated, interesting . . . why quibble! But seriously, let's see if we can straighten this out a bit, see what makes sense and what doesn't.

I was following pretty well up to the point of the contract and God's dilemma. And I can see that the devil would assume Jesus is human and therefore part of his team and someone who would die. Finally, I get that Jesus, if he didn't sin, wouldn't actually deserve to die. But how that all works out is beyond me. For instance, why does Jesus' dying affect the rest of us?

That's a great question, and there's more than one way to answer it.

More than one way?

Yeah, let's keep in mind that this way of thinking about the cross is developed and employed over a thousand years, and so there are a lot of variations. That will be true of all three of the theories we identified. What we're really doing is grouping a number of variations together into three schools, or models, based on their similarities.

And so what makes this "classic" school of ideas similar?

They all agree on the dilemma: humans have sinned, so the devil has claim to them, and Jesus' death frees them from that claim.

Okay, but how? Or is that where the variations come in?

It is. One variation—proposed by one of the first theologians of the church, a guy named Origen—was that God actually arranged with the devil to give Satan his Son (Jesus) as payment, or as a ransom, for all of humanity. The idea was that Satan, given the opportunity to have control over God's Son, would jump at this chance, because by controlling the Son, he could gain a lot of leverage over the Father.

Wait . . . God "pays" the devil with Jesus?

Right. Jesus is the ransom God pays the devil for the rest of humanity. Origen and others look especially to Mark's Gospel, where Jesus says, "For the Son of Man came not to be served but to serve, and to give his life a ransom for many" (10:45). And there's a verse in one of the letters in the New Testament that has a similar theme: "For there is one God; there is also one mediator between God and humankind, Christ Jesus, himself human, who gave himself a ransom for all" (1 Timothy 2:5-6).

Huh. I'd never heard those verses about ransom before. Are there other verses like that?

Not really. And, to tell you the truth, there's little indication that when Mark wrote his Gospel that's the kind of ransom he meant.

But then why do they build their understanding of the cross on such a small part of the Bible?

There are other parts of the New Testament that portray Jesus' death as a struggle, and there are whole sections, such as the book of Revelation, that describe the cosmic struggle between God and the devil. But you're right. On the whole, this theory isn't built on specific passages from the Bible but instead on general themes.

But Christians still found it helpful?

You have to keep in mind that when we try to make sense of the cross, we're often saying as much about ourselves—our situation, our questions, our struggles—as we are about the cross. Many early Christians found confessing faith in Jesus a struggle. They were sometimes persecuted and at times died for their faith. So it makes some sense that they would understand Jesus' cross as representing a larger struggle between God and the devil and look to those portions of Scripture to help them understand both the cross and their lives.

That's helpful. Thanks.

Okay, so let me see if I am following. Because of the sin of Adam and Eve and the rest of us, the devil holds humanity hostage, and God offers Jesus as a ransom. The devil accepts, thinking that he'd rather have the Son of God than all of humanity, because that puts him in a pretty good position to get what he wants from God.

Right.

So why doesn't it work? Why doesn't the devil end up on top?

Because death and the devil can't hold Jesus.

And Jesus knew this?

That's hard to tell. I think the emphasis of these early Christians was that God knew this and so entered into the agreement to free humanity, but it's not clear whether or not Jesus, as a human as well as the Son of God, knew this ahead of time or just entered into it trusting his fate to God.

But if God knew this ahead of time, it almost sounds like God tricked the devil.

That's actually one of the ways early Christians described it. It seemed fair to them, because the devil had tricked Adam and Eve in the first place, telling them that if they ate the fruit they wouldn't die but would become like God. And so God, you might say, beats the devil at his own game by tricking him into accepting Jesus as a ransom.

You know, this all seems weirdly familiar somehow, although it's hard to see why.

Did you ever read C. S. Lewis's *The Lion, the Witch and the Wardrobe*?

Yeah, it was one of my favorites as a kid, though it's been a long time since I read it.

That story might be why this one seems familiar. This is the theory that Lewis more or less uses in his story. In *The Lion, the Witch and the Wardrobe*, Edmund, who's called a "son of Adam," sides with the White Witch because she promises to make him a king.

I remember that. She's pretty scary, and I can see how she's sort of like the devil tricking Adam and Eve, or in this case a son of Adam, into sinning.

Right, and once Edmund goes over, she has a claim on him and is free to kill him. So the great lion Aslan . . .

Who represents Jesus, right?

Right. Aslan offers to trade himself for Edmund.

As a ransom. I think I see.

As a ransom, yes. And the witch accepts, believing that once Aslan's out of the way, she can come back and kill Edmund and the rest anyway.

But Aslan doesn't stay dead. And so he foils all her plans.

Exactly.

Yeah, I can see how this is the theory that inspires Lewis.

Does it make a little more sense?

Yeah, I think so, with emphasis on *little*. But, to be frank, I can't say I like this picture of God tricking the devil. I mean, it's one thing for the devil to go around tricking people—that's what we expect from the devil. But it's another for God to be doing it.

You're not alone in thinking that. In fact, that's where one of the other main variations comes into play.

I'm all ears.

In this case, the emphasis isn't so much on tricking the devil as it is on Jesus embracing the full human condition, including death, and winning a victory over it.

How does he do that?

In this version, the main enemy isn't just the devil but death itself. And so Jesus enters into human life, knowing full well that he will die. In fact, he knows that precisely because he *is* God in the flesh the devil—whose chief weapon is death—will come after him. And that's what happens. Jesus comes, and the devil, working through the people in power who are threatened by Jesus, puts him to death on the cross. It looks very much like the devil's won when Jesus dies, but in the end Jesus is raised from death, and so death and the devil no longer have a claim on him.

I can see how that's great for Jesus, but how does it help us?

Because, as the apostle Paul says at one point, we are joined in baptism to Jesus, both his death and his resurrection (Romans 6:3-4). So because we're joined to Jesus through faith, just as he shared our death, we will eventually share his resurrection.

And he had to die for all this to happen?

Right. The only way he could defeat death was first to embrace it. There's just no way around the human condition, and death is perhaps the darkest element of that condition. But once he's died—that is, death has done its worst to him—and then he's raised, it's clear that he's stronger even than death, and so all those who are united to him through faith will also be raised from death.

This reminds me of another movie, actually.

Which one?

***Stars Wars*, where Obi-Wan Kenobi meets Darth Vader and they're dueling and Vader's pretty sure he has the upper hand. And then Obi-Wan says, "You can't win, Darth. If you strike me down, I shall become more powerful than you could possibly imagine."**

That's right. In this sense, the cross is like a mighty struggle between God, in Jesus, and death itself. And the only way to defeat death is to embrace it, to actually go through it and come out on the other side resurrected. So, like Obi-Wan, Jesus is struck down in order that he—and all of us—might become more powerful, that is, no longer subject to death and the devil.

Well, I think I like this version a little better. At least God's not a trickster. And I like the emphasis on the cross as a life-and-death struggle. That certainly rings true to Mark and Matthew's portrayals of the very real pain and agony of the cross. And the idea that what looks like defeat—the cross—ends up being victory seems a whole lot like Mark's idea that God comes to us where we least expect God to be.

I think you're right.

You know what, though? I actually think it also matches up somewhat with John's vision of the cross as well. This emphasis on victory reminds me of how, in John, Jesus not only embraces death confidently but in the end shouts out that his mission has been accomplished.

I think you're right. There are definitely tones of John's sense of victory, too. In fact, this version, in addition to being called the classic or ransom theory of atonement, has sometimes been called the *Christus Victor* or the "Victorious Christ" theory of atonement. It was developed in part by some other early Christians and then revived by a Swedish theologian named Gustaf Aulén in the middle of the twentieth century.

Really? So it's not only the ancient Christians who believed this, but some people believe it today?

Aulén argued that it was the theory that the sixteenth-century Reformers adopted, though others disagree. In all honesty, I'd say that over the last few centuries, it's been most influential in the Greek and Russian Orthodox churches, though they see it as more metaphorical than actual.

What do you mean?

They see the themes of ransom and victory as symbolizing how God entered into human life and freed us from death, sin, and the devil. But they don't get too hung up on how it actually happened.

That's helpful, to think of it symbolically, especially when I remember what you said about how some of the earliest Christians really struggled and even were persecuted for their faith.

And that's sometimes still true today.

What do you mean?

Just that other Christians, especially those living under oppression, have more recently recovered the symbolism of the classic theory of atonement as well. Sometimes it might be economic or political oppression, while at other times it might be because they are the minority religious group in their homeland. Or it might be that they are struggling with addiction or trapped in an abusive relationship. Christians in any of these situations might see these forces of oppression and misery as linked to death and the devil, and they may feel very much that they are being held hostage by the forces of evil. So the imagery of Jesus taking on their situation, their death, and struggling to free them is pretty powerful.

Yeah, I can see that. And I can see how to someone who feels trapped or held hostage this would be a very important picture of what Jesus accomplishes through the cross.

Even with that in mind, though, I still find it hard to, you know, embrace it myself.

Why do you think that is?

I guess it's like you said up front: this is just a very different way of thinking about things—about life, about the world, about God. It all seems pretty foreign to me, although it's hard to describe it all.

Maybe it will help to go back to the four categories we talked about earlier.

I think that's a good idea.

So we nailed down the problem earlier, the "what needs to be fixed"—it's that death and the devil have a claim on us because of sin.

Right. And—second question—how does God do that?

By coming in the person of Jesus to win us back, either by tricking the devil into a "bait and switch"—Satan thinks he's getting God's favorite human but really is getting God in human form—or by entering into the darkest and most difficult element of human life and coming out on the other side victorious.

Very good. And the picture of God?

I guess the picture of God is of one who wants to win us back. In fact, God wants us back so badly that God is willing to do just about anything— tricking the devil in the one scenario and struggling to the death in the cross in the other.

What about our lives in this world? What does this theory of atonement say about how we should live our lives?

It doesn't seem to say a whole lot, actually. I mean, I can't see how this theory does a lot to help me think about what it means to be Christian, except maybe to be grateful that I'm not the devil's hostage anymore.

I hear what you're saying, though I think the folks who live with this model would suggest it can influence our lives profoundly.

In what way?

Now that we are free from the clutches of the devil, we are also free—in fact, we *need*—to stand against the forces of evil that once enslaved us. That is, now that we're back on God's "team," we are called to resist oppression, addiction, tyranny, and all the rest wherever we see them.

Very interesting. And that actually reminds me of something else.

What's that?

Well, in talking about the Christian life, it reminded me of when you said that Jesus' life not only helps explain the cross, but that the cross also helps to make sense of Jesus' life.

Yes?

It occurred to me that this theory doesn't seem to deal with Jesus' life much at all. I mean, do the things he said and did matter, or do things only get interesting when he goes to the cross?

That's a great question. Actually, Jesus' whole life on earth signals a lifelong struggle with the devil, a struggle that reaches its climax with the cross.

How so?

First, the fact that God would enter into human life is pretty incredible. The perfect joins the imperfect; the eternal takes on the finite; the incorruptible embraces the corrupted. God's taking our form in Christ is a huge event in and of itself.

Second, each miracle of Jesus was a way of asserting that sin and death don't have the last word. That God's desire for creation is health, not sickness; abundance, not hunger; and so forth. Especially when Jesus heals people who are possessed, you can see him challenging the authority of the devil.

That's very interesting, and probably another reason this theory is comforting to people who are struggling, whether with oppression or illness or whatever.

Life, at times, just plain feels like a struggle, and I can see how it would help to believe that our struggle isn't all there is, that somehow Jesus has entered into it and was victorious.

I think that's quite insightful.

Thanks.

Having said that, though, I think you're also right. This theory doesn't grow out of a close reading of the Gospels or deal a whole lot with the particulars of Jesus' life. It takes those elements as a starting point, but then it projects more particular concerns about life and death and the eternal struggle between good and evil onto those details.

You know, that helps me name a point I'm still stuck on.

What's that?

Just that in the end it feels so, I don't know, mythological, maybe even theoretical. It's kind of a great story, pretty dramatic and all that—especially the version that emphasizes victory rather than just tricking the devil—but it doesn't ever really touch me.

Can you say a little more?

Sure. Maybe it's because I haven't suffered persecution the way the early Christians did. But I guess it just feels a little out there—not just in terms of being a bit far-fetched for a modern person to understand, but more in terms of it being a story about what God did that never really affects me, never makes a difference to me, never makes any kind of claim on me. I can listen to it and find it interesting or unbelievable or whatever, but it still seems like this huge story about the cosmic battle between good and evil that somehow never really quite gets under my skin and does anything to me.

I think I see what you mean.

Remember when we said that part of the way we'll decide which of these different theories is right, or at least better, is how it makes us feel? How it explains things in a way that not only makes sense, but also makes a difference to us? Well, I think that's what's lacking here. It kind of explains things—though in a way that's still hard to wrap my modern mind around—but it doesn't in the end make much of a difference to my everyday life. At least, not

most of the time.

That's a good caution to keep in mind. If we are facing extreme challenges and life seems to be conspiring against us, then this picture of God jumping into the fray and coming to our side to help us may be quite powerful. At the same time, it's so cosmic and mythic in scope that it runs the risk of being seen primarily as kind of a cool drama, in the *Stars Wars* way of things, that rarely touches or shapes our everyday lives all that much.

Yeah. So while I really like the emphasis on struggle and victory, maybe it's time to move on to the next understanding of atonement.

Sounds like a good idea.

Insights and Questions

CHAPTER 4

Substitution, Satisfaction, and Sacrifice

So you said that the classic theory of atonement that focuses on ransom and victory was popular for about a thousand years or so. The second theory—what did you say that is about?

Substitution, satisfaction, and sacrifice.

That's kind of a mouthful.

It is. We'll unpack it in a bit. For now, it's probably enough to think in terms of substitution, because that's what becomes most important.

Okay. So does this second theory, about substitution, come up after the first one loses steam?

Yes, the substitution theory of atonement was formulated not only *after* the ransom theory, but also very much as a *reaction* to it. In fact, the ransom theory began to go out of vogue in large part because the substitution theory seems to explain things better for later generations of Christians.

So these later Christians didn't like the ransom theory.

No. In particular, a theologian by the name of Anselm had huge problems with it, so he formulated another theory.

What are Anselm's complaints?

Actually, they're pretty similar to the ones you named. In particular, he thinks it's way, way beneath God's honor and dignity to go around tricking the devil.

I knew it!

Yeah, Anselm totally agrees. In fact, God's honor is a huge thing for Anselm, so he uses his sense of God's honor not only to critique the classic ransom view, but also to formulate his own.

Interesting. Can you say a little more?

Sure. It might be helpful first to give a little background about Anselm and the world he lived in.

Sounds good.

Anselm was born in 1033 to a noble family. From a very early age, he wanted to become a monk. He eventually became not only a monk, but the abbot, or leader, of a famous monastery. He was later made Archbishop of Canterbury, which was a very important position. During all those years he regularly negotiated with the kings of his day regarding the authority of the church and its relationship to the crown. He also wrote a number of important theological treatises (essays), one trying to prove the existence of God and another, as we'll see, about the meaning and significance of the cross.

Sounds like he was a busy guy.

Very.

And it's his work about the cross that we're going to talk about?

Yes, although it's important not to forget his lifelong struggle with the monarchy.

Why?

Because it reminds us of maybe the most important thing about Anselm to keep in mind when we take up his theology: he lived during the Middle Ages, during the feudal era when kings ruled the world and there was an absolute hierarchy to all social relationships.

Why is that so important?

Because we live in a democracy, and it's just really, really hard for us to grasp how completely the people of the medieval world were divided into social classes. The distinctions between a king and a peasant weren't merely economic, like those between someone in our country who is very wealthy and someone who is very poor. They were absolute. Monarchs—kings mostly, at this time, but eventually queens—were of a totally different order than peasants. There was a clear boundary between common people and royalty, and there was no way of crossing the divide. Peasants owed the king everything. In a very real sense, kings owned peasants.

That doesn't seem right.

Not to us. But the Middle Ages were a pretty difficult time to live, and this kind of absolute class structure helped keep some semblance of order and a measure of security. Kings protected peasants; in return, peasants owed their king absolute loyalty and obedience. Any disobedience or disloyalty therefore called for immediate and severe punishment.

And how does all this come back to our discussion about the meaning of the cross?

In his writing, Anselm assumes an analogous relationship between God and humanity. God is, in a very real sense to Anselm, our divine and cosmic king. We owe absolutely everything to God.

I'm not sure what exactly the problem is. I mean, isn't that what most Christians believe, that we owe everything to God? We're not talking about an earthly king, after all; we're talking about God.

Right. The most important thing about Anselm's argument, at this point, isn't that he thinks we owe everything to God, but that God is like a king. In particular, that God is like a medieval king.

I'm not sure I've caught the distinction you're making.

We might agree with Anselm that we owe God everything and should obey God in all things, but when we don't follow through, when we sin, we probably wouldn't say the problem is that we've offended God's honor.

And that's what Anselm says?

Yes, because he's thinking in medieval terms about a king's honor. For instance, do you remember when I said that Anselm rejects the classical theory because he is offended at the notion that God enters into a contract with the devil and, even more, that God owes the devil payment?

Sure. And, quite frankly, I agree with him. It just sounds, I don't know, *beneath* God to have to even negotiate with the devil, let alone to have God resort to tricking the devil.

Right. Anselm agrees. He doesn't actually mind the ransom and victory understandings of the cross when we take them symbolically— kind of as *simple pictures* to help people understand the importance of the cross or God's determination to win us back—but he thinks they're completely inadequate as *explanations* of the cross. They just can't explain why the cross had to happen. And that's Anselm's big question: why?

But that's my question—the question we started with!

Anselm's, too. In fact, he names his major work on the cross *Cur Deus Homo?*—or, *Why the God Man*? Anselm wants to know why God had to become human and, even more, why God had to die on the cross. And to explain that, he emphasizes God's divine royalty and the debt of honor we owe God.

Okay, back to the honor thing. Well, I thought I was with you for a while, but now I'm not so sure.

We've said that it somehow doesn't seem right for God to have to trick the devil. Why? Because it's beneath God's honor. God, after all, is God, and like a medieval king, God deserves the respect, loyalty, allegiance, and obedience of *all* creatures, including the devil, as well as every single person.

I think I'm following.

Well, the problem is that every time we sin we *don't* give God the honor that we owe God as the one who created us and gave us life. Sin, essentially, is disobedience, disloyalty, a withholding of the honor due God that creates a kind of moral imbalance in the universe.

So to put it in the terms we discussed earlier, that's the problem for Anselm, the thing that's broken. We have not given God the honor that God deserves.

Right, except it's even worse. Not only have we not given God the honor God deserves, but we can *never* make it up to God. First, because we're sinful, we don't seem capable of living a sinless life and honoring God the way we should. And, second, nothing we do, once we've sinned, is good, worthy, or important enough to pay back the debt of honor we owe. That is, if we already owe God everything, there's nothing left over that we can do that would make up for our sins, and therefore no way to restore the moral order.

That means we're in a serious bind.

Which is exactly the conclusion Anselm comes to. And that, for him, explains why God became human and died on the cross.

All right. We need to slow down again. So, Anselm believes that humanity has not given God the honor God deserves, and, further, there is no way for humanity to pay this debt.

Right.

And, according to Anselm, God is like a king; actually, God is the King of the universe, and people are more like peasants, the cosmic King's subjects.

Right again.

That all makes sense. But I'm still not sure how the cross solves this problem.

That's where the title of Anselm's book becomes important: *Why the God Man*? Anselm looks to the incarnation, the Christian belief that

Jesus is both fully God and fully human, and he finds a solution to the problem he's posed.

I'm all ears.

Well, the problem is sort of an accounting problem.

Say that again?

I know that sounds odd. But it actually makes sense. After all, think how many times we've talked about "debts" and "owing" and the like. These are essentially accounting terms. We *owe* God everything. We haven't *given* God everything God deserves. There is, therefore, a *debt* of honor that we can't pay God. More than that, we'll never be able to *pay* God everything, which means we'll always be in *debt*.

Okay, that makes sense; the accounting part, that is. I'm still not sure how Jesus solves this.

The problem is that we humans owe God an infinite debt, one we'll never be able to repay because we are only human. As it turns out, only God could possibly pay God back.

So why doesn't God just do that? Why doesn't God just pay God's own self back? I mean, can't God just forgive us? Why wouldn't that work?

Because that would wreck the whole system. Let's go back to accounting for a second. You can't have a bank loaning money to a bunch of people and then deciding that they don't have to pay it back. The bank would go out of business. And you can't have the bank deciding that only some people have to pay back their loans, either, because that wouldn't be fair. You wouldn't be able to trust the bank.

To Anselm, it's pretty much the same problem with God. You can't just have God pay God back by forgiving us or by forgetting about the sin, because God, as a king, is first and foremost just. And so God also has to play by the rules. The rules of justice demand some kind of payment to restore the moral order.

So it almost sounds like the problem is as much God's as it is humans'.

That's right, and this will be important to remember. God very much wants to be merciful to humans, but God is in a bind. God made the rules that govern the universe and God can't just go and break them. So humans owe God a debt, and there are only two ways this debt can be paid: either by satisfaction—humans making payment—or by death. Remember, disloyalty to the king demands death.

MORE?!

Because if the king just goes around forgiving people, no one will bother obeying him.

Right.

And if the king forgives some people and not others, that wouldn't be fair, and you wouldn't be able to trust the king.

Yes.

This all reminds me of another story.

Really?

Yeah, especially the part about medieval kings. Remember King Arthur?

Sure. It's a great story. And I think the Arthur stories were popularized around the time Anselm was writing.

Maybe that explains the connection. Because while most of the story of King Arthur is great, there's one particularly heartbreaking part, when Lancelot, Arthur's best knight and closest friend, and Guinevere, Arthur's wife and queen, betray him by having an affair.

Oh yeah. That is heartbreaking.

Especially because Arthur still loves each of them. I mean, he's totally wrecked by what they do, but he can't help loving them still. At the same time, they've totally betrayed him and, more importantly, broken the law.

So what does he do? I don't quite remember.

That's what this reminded me of. At one point—and I can't remember if this is in the book or one of the movies made about the story—he says that as a man he would easily forgive each of them, even bless them to be with each other because he loves them so much. But as a king he can't do that. As a king he must punish them. Otherwise, the king's justice wouldn't mean anything.
That sounds exactly like the bind Anselm imagines God being in.

That *is* exactly the bind Anselm imagines God being in. Because God is a king, God must demand justice—payment of the debt—either by satisfaction or punishment, which in this case is eternal death.

And this is where Jesus comes in?

Right. Because Jesus is God, Jesus can pay God back. And because Jesus is human, that payment counts as ours.

Can you say a little more about each of those two parts—Jesus as God and Jesus as human?

Sure, let's start with Jesus as God. Because Jesus is God's Son, Jesus is perfectly obedient. In fact, he's more than obedient. He not only lives a sinless life, but he actually goes to the cross and dies out of his devotion to God. He renders complete honor to God, and his death is even more than God would normally expect and so must be rewarded. Jesus can then share that reward with all humanity. He can render God sufficient honor that not only satisfies what God deserves, but also leaves enough left over to cover what we owe as well.

Okay, I'm with you.

Because Jesus is also human, his payment counts as ours. That is, Jesus is able to serve as a substitute for us. Again, God can't simply pay our debt—that wouldn't be fair—but Jesus, as a human, can pay back the debt for us.

So let me see if I've got this. Because Jesus is God, his obedient death on the cross satisfies God's honor; it's enough to pay back the debt owed to God. And because Jesus is human, his payment can substitute for ours.

Right.

And that, to answer Anselm's question, is why there is a God-man and, even more, why the God-man dies on the cross—because Jesus is sent by God to pay the debt that we can't pay.

Right again.

Okay, I think I've got it. And, to be honest, it actually makes a lot of sense. More than that, it also seems that Anselm wants to stress that God loves us. I wasn't so sure for a little while.

What do you mean?

Well, with all this emphasis on God's honor, you can begin to get the idea that what's most important to God is God's honor, not us. But now it seems more like God's caught in the same system we are, and so because God loves us, God figures out a way to save us—by sending the God-man, Jesus.

That's right. There are some touching parts of Anselm's book where he actually imagines God talking about how much God loves us and sending Jesus to save us because of that love.

I think that's important. And, again, it helps complete Anselm's theory. When you think about it, he's really figured out a way to solve the puzzle without any pieces left over.

That's what made Anselm's theory so popular. Everything adds up.

And that's the theory most Christians believe today?

A lot of Christians do, although the story doesn't quite end here.

How does it continue?

Anselm's thought became quite popular very quickly because it seemed to answer the question of why the cross was necessary in terms everyone can understand. As we'll see in a bit, it didn't satisfy everyone, but by and large it became the accepted teaching about the cross in the Western, Roman Catholic, and, later, Protestant world. But two more theologians developed it, and it's this developed theory that is most popular today.

Who are these theologians, and what did they change?

Their names are Thomas Aquinas and John Calvin. They didn't really change anything in the basic formulation that Anselm came up with, but they did shift the emphasis a bit.

In what way?

They shifted the emphasis from God's honor to payment for sin.

How do you mean?

In Anselm, what humanity owes God is a debt of honor. But in Aquinas and Calvin, it's not so much God's honor that has been offended as it is God's justice. So what's necessary isn't simply obedience—to restore the debt of honor—but punishment. The only way that the penalty for sin can be paid is for those sins to be punished. So what happens on the cross isn't just that Jesus is obedient and is therefore rewarded for his obedience, but that Jesus is actually being punished in our place. Later this became known as *penal substitution*. Jesus is being punished as a substitute for us.

That's pretty intense, although in some ways it makes a little more sense to me than the whole thing about God's honor. I mean, that's kind of like our saying, "If you do the crime, you do the time." Except that Jesus steps in and does the time—takes our punishment—for us.

Right.

So Aquinas and Calvin both came up with this?

Aquinas was first. He was born in 1225. According to him, Jesus is being punished for original sin, and individual humans need to take care of their own sins through confession and penance.

Confession and penance?

In Roman Catholic tradition, especially in the Middle Ages but still in some respects today, you need to go to the priest and confess your sins. And then the priest gives you something to do—like saying the Lord's Prayer or making a donation to charity—to make up for your sins. Aquinas actually did a lot both to make Anselm's teaching, adapted slightly, the central teaching of the Roman Catholic Church, and to establish the whole medieval system of confession, penance, and absolution that was ultimately based on it.

And what about Calvin?

Calvin, who was born in 1509, was one of the Protestant Reformers and a younger contemporary of Martin Luther. He didn't believe we need penance, because, like Luther, he believed that we are completely justified, or made right with God, by faith apart from any works. So he taught that Christ was being punished on the cross both for original sin and for all of our later sins.

That language about sin sounds familiar.

The apostle Paul at one point says, "Christ died for our sins" (1 Corinthians 15:3). At another point, he states it even more strongly: writing God put forth Jesus "as a sacrifice for atonement" (Romans 3:25). And in John's Gospel, Jesus is called "the lamb of God who takes away the sin of the world" (John 1:29).

Right. I knew I'd heard that before. And is that what Paul and John meant? I mean, Aquinas and Calvin seem to have taken it quite literally.

That's a great question. And we'll want to look at those passages more closely a little later. For now, it's important to recognize that they do, indeed, not only take Paul and John quite literally but also read them in light of their own sense of God's justice and the accounting system they've used to explain the cross. The main point, for them, is that Jesus didn't die because of our sins in general, but actually as a result of his substituting for us and actually bearing the punishment and death for our sins that we deserve.

And, according to Aquinas, Calvin, and later theologians, this means that we don't have to be punished?

Right. The key for Calvin, in particular, is accepting and believing that Jesus was being punished for us. If you do, then you can enjoy the benefits of Christ's substitutionary death.

Wow. That's a pretty complete system.

Yeah, it is. Again, I think both the simplicity and the completeness of Anselm's thought, adapted and extended by Aquinas and Calvin, is what has made it so popular.

But I'm curious to know what you think.

Well, like I said, on a lot of levels it makes sense. We're used to thinking about crime and punishment. That's the way our whole legal system works. And if you accept the way Anselm described the problem, it all hangs together quite nicely. We have offended God's honor (or, later, justice) and can't pay the

debt. Because Jesus is God, he can pay it (or be punished for us), and because Jesus is human, it can count for us.

Great summary.

It's actually not hard to remember, because there's a serious logic to the whole thing, and to be honest, that's pretty appealing.
But I think that's also what troubles me.

The logic? Would you rather have something be *illogical*?

No. Or maybe yes. I'm not sure how to say it.

This is complicated stuff. Just try your best, and we'll figure it out together.

Okay, so here's the thing: I actually do like that it's logical. It all adds up—like accounting. But that's also the problem. Life isn't like accounting. I mean, some parts are—when we use our credit cards, take out a loan to buy a house, and all that. But the most important parts of life aren't about debits and credits; they're about relationships. I can't imagine running my personal life like a bank does its business.

What do you mean?

Think about it: keeping track of what everyone owes you and what you owe everyone else. Making sure that every offense, every slight, every injury is accounted for and duly punished. You'd drive yourself—and everyone around you—nuts if you tried.

I think I see what you mean. This may work for accounting, but not for relationships.

Exactly. Could you imagine if your parents made sure you paid for every misstep you made?

I'd still be paying.

Or if you decided that's the way you'd relate to your kids? They'd absolutely hate you.

But don't you think that's what Anselm and company were trying to convey? Not so much a detailed list of credits and debits, but an overall sense of just how bad our situation is and why it took Jesus' death on the cross to straighten things out.

I can see that, especially with Anselm, who did, after all, want to show us how much God loves us. But it's the larger accounting system that Anselm and the rest seem to employ that's still a problem. On the one hand it, makes sense. Like I said, it's logical. But on the other hand, I have to wonder why God gets caught up in the same accounting system we use. After all, God is God, for crying out loud!

I think I see what you mean. And, now that you mention it, it ends up not being all that different than the ransom system.

What do you mean?

Well, we said that we didn't like this idea that God had to pay the devil something. But Anselm solved it by saying that God has to pay *God* something. I mean, humanity actually is the one who has to pay God, but . . .

Since humanity can't pay it, and since God loves us, it becomes God's problem, and God has to find a way to pay God back. I see what you mean.

Right, and while maybe that's better than God having to negotiate with the devil, God is still caught up in some kind of system of debits and credits.

Which brings me back to the question: why can't God just forgive us? I understand why Anselm thought God can't do that, though I'm not sure I agree. We're not in a business relationship with God; we're in a personal relationship, and in personal relationships people forgive each other all the time. Which I guess names for me the problem I have with this theory.

Say a little more.

Well, it's definitely logical, but it's the kind of cold, calculating logic of business, of accounting, of credits and debits, not the logic of personal relationships and family.
    Don't get me wrong—some of my best friends are accountants! So I understand why we need accounting, and I'm all for calculations when it comes to our business transactions. I'm just not so sure it's what we need

when it comes to our personal relationships with the people we love and live with.

> I think I see what you mean. And I agree with you. As much as Anselm may want to stress God's love, it still comes down to a fairly impersonal and calculating system that ultimately traps not just humanity, but God.

Maybe that made sense in the medieval world of kings and peasants and justice and all that. But I don't think it matches my idea of God.

> You're right. In the Bible God is described as a king, but it's usually a protective, caring king more than the medieval sense of a king. And God is also described as being a loving parent.

It just seems like the loving nature of God gets lost with Aquinas and Calvin.

> How so?

Well, in Anselm's picture of things, God loves us but is caught in the same system of honor and justice we are. When you get to Aquinas and Calvin, though, suddenly it's hard to imagine that God even really loves us.

> Say a little more.

Like you said, it's not just about Jesus being obedient and more than satisfying God's honor anymore; now it's about punishment. Because of sin, someone has to be punished. Someone has to die. Quite frankly, from this point of view, God seems just plain ticked off.

> Theologians would call that "the wrath of God"—God's just anger at our sin.

I guess that makes sense. But is the wrath of God a big part of the Bible?

> Actually, no, it's not. It's clearly there; that is, there are places in the Bible where God is depicted as angry—usually when we are mistreating each other. But, on the whole, it's not a major theme, and most often the phrase "the wrath of God" is used to describe what seems like a passive, rather than active, attribute of God.

I'm not sure I understand.

It's like the world is set up so that when you don't obey God's laws, you suffer the natural consequences. The "wrath of God," in this sense, describes what happens when you go against the laws of nature God put in place. But it's usually not that God is just plain angry and wants to get us, let alone that God wants to get revenge on us.

But here, that's just the way it seems. Or, at least it seems that God can't *really* love us or forgive us until there's been some bloodshed.

I think Calvin and Aquinas would both want to stress, with Anselm, that God *has* to punish us, not because God doesn't love us but because God is just, and if God isn't just, then we probably shouldn't trust this God. Moreover, they would argue that justice *is* a form of love, a way of ordering the world so that it is fair and trustworthy.

But does God's justice have to be satisfied by having someone punished *before* God can love us?

I think Calvin and Aquinas at many points in their writings say that God loves us all along, but by our actions we deserve only punishment, so God, to be a just God, has to punish us, or at least punish Jesus in our place, before God can forgive us.

But that's just the problem. Okay, sure, God loves us. But not really. I mean, God can't act toward us in a loving way until there's been punishment. It's like there are two things that are central about God: God is loving *and* God is just. But when push comes to shove, God is more *just* than God is *loving*. Or, to put it another way, first God has to be just, and only then can God be loving. Either way you put it, God's justice trumps God's love.

I see what you mean.

This all actually reminds me of another story. With Anselm, the King Arthur story worked to describe the bind God's in. But once we turn to Aquinas and Calvin, it reminds me more of Charles Dickens's story about the French Revolution, *A Tale of Two Cities*.

Okay, so I read that in high school and all, but I have to admit that it's been a long time and I can't say I remember it too well.

I'm not that surprised; it's a huge and complicated book. But I can give you

a quick recap of the essential scene. It comes right near the end of the book and involves two main characters. The first is Charles Darnay, a Frenchman who has renounced his aristocratic heritage but has been sentenced to death for the crimes of his father and uncle. Darnay, in fact, is awaiting execution in this scene.

So he's the character that represents humanity.

Right. And then there's Sydney Carton, the second character. He's a lawyer, and he's not only Darnay's friend, but he looks almost exactly like him. But Carton's also in love with Darnay's wife, and he's something of a drunk.

Don't tell me—Carton represents Jesus. I mean, I get the parallel in that Carton looks just like Darnay and can stand in for him, but I don't know, if he's a drunk and all . . .

Look, I didn't say this was a perfect analogy; I said it reminded me of what we're talking about.

Right. Sorry about that.

No problem.

Okay, so there we are: Darnay is about to be executed. The situation is pretty hopeless, as there's no way the French revolutionaries are going to forgive him for the crimes his family committed. But that night Carton comes to his friend's cell and tricks him into changing clothes with him. Then he drugs Darnay and has someone sneak him out of prison while he, Carton, stays behind. The next day, as Darnay and his wife escape Paris, Carton is executed in Darnay's place.

I see the connection to the substitutionary atonement. Carton dies in Darnay's place.

Right, but what's interesting is what happens when you extend the analogy. You already got us started. Darnay is like us, condemned to die. Carton is like Jesus, looking just like us and so a perfect substitute. But who's the character that stands in for God, you know, the one who demands punishment for past wrongs?

The French revolutionaries!

That's right—it's the ravenous crowd who won't be satisfied until someone

dies. I mean, according to their sense of justice, blood has to be shed to make up for the crimes of the past.

That's kind of a frightening analogy.

Again, I know it's not perfect.

But it does bring out the problem with this theory of atonement. At its best, it assumes that God can't deal directly with the problem of sin or redeem us. At it's worst, this theory seems to imply that God is just plain angry and nothing can satisfy God's wrath except for the blood of an innocent victim.

Like I said, it may be logical, but it's a cold, calculating logic that doesn't end up portraying God in a very good light.

Moreover, that's not the picture of God in the Bible.

I'm glad to hear it. But can you say a little more?

There's talk of ransom in the Bible, like we said, and talk of sacrifice and the like as well. But it's never a sacrifice made to God to satisfy God's wrath. God, according to Jesus, is primarily about love. According to the apostle Paul, in fact, "God proves his love for us in that while we were still sinners Christ died for us" (Romans 5:8).

You mentioned that we would come back to Paul. But what does he mean by that? I like the way it sounds, but I'm not sure I understand.

Well, it's pretty much like what you were saying. It's not that God's justice has to be satisfied in order for God to love us. God loves us all along the way. In fact, for Paul the cross doesn't make it possible for God to love and forgive us; the cross is actually the sign that God *already* loves and forgives us.

So God *can* forgive us?

According to Paul and the Gospel stories we looked at, God is forgiving all the time. That's what gets Jesus into trouble in the first place—he goes around forgiving everyone.

That's a really helpful point. But what about all those things about Jesus dying for our sins or being offered as a sacrifice?

That's where things get interesting. Let's look a little closer at the passage where Paul says that God put Jesus forth as a sacrifice for atonement. The Greek word that gets translated here as "atonement"—the New Testament was written in Greek—can be translated in a couple of ways. The folks who favor the penal substitutionary theory of atonement translate it as "propitiation", which describes the sacrifice people in the ancient world would make to appease an angry diety.

You mean like satisfying God's wrath, kind of like we said Aquinas and Calvin had been saying?

Right. But another way to translate the word is "expiation", which means simply to make pure or take away sin; or atonement. This meaning goes back to the Hebrew word behind this one.

I thought you said the New Testament was written in Greek.

You're right, I did; and it is. But the Old Testament is written in Hebrew and later translated into Greek, and Paul knows this Greek version of the Old Testament, so sometimes it's helpful to see what Hebrew word lies behind the Greek one he uses in his writings.

If you say so . . .

Trust me on this one. The heart of the matter, though, is that the Hebrew word behind the Greek one Paul is using really means a "hiding" or "covering over" of our sin.

Which sounds like forgiveness!

Exactly.

You're right, that is very interesting. And what about John, where he describes Jesus as the Lamb of God?

Again, that's pretty interesting. We're inclined to read any sacrifice as one made to appease an angry god. But the original Passover story that stands behind John's story isn't that kind of sacrifice at all.

Passover. That's right. I remember you saying that John described Jesus as being crucified at the exact moment the Passover lambs were sacrificed.

Right. But the Passover sacrifice was never intended to appease God's anger; instead, it was to remember when God literally "passed over" the houses of the Israelites and struck only the Egyptians on the night God delivered the Israelites from slavery.

So the sacrifice, in this case, was to remember God's mercy and deliverance. Which, again, sounds closer to forgiveness than it does punishment.

I agree.

That would seem, then, to raise a very important question.

What's that?

Well, with all of this talk of honor and justice and punishment and the like, where *is* God's forgiveness in the substitutionary theory of atonement? I mean, did they just forget about that? *Can* God forgive us apart from the cross or not?

Again, I think Anselm, Aquinas, and Calvin would want to be careful not to say that it's the cross that makes it *possible* for God to forgive us. Rather, they'd want to say that the cross is how God actually *enacts* forgiveness. That is, the cross is the means by which the God-man, Jesus, pays the debt or is punished in our place. It's what forgiveness looks like.

Except it's *not* what forgiveness looks like. I mean, is it really forgiveness if Jesus had to pay for it? Think about it: if I loan you money, and you can't pay me back, so I find someone who can, I didn't forgive you anything. I just helped you pay it back. Maybe that's nice, but it's not forgiveness. In fact, it's a lot closer to foreclosure.

What do you mean?

Just that if you take out a mortgage and can't pay it, the bank may renegotiate your loan or give you an extension, but eventually, if you can't pay, they take back your house and sell it to try to pay off your loan. That's foreclosure, something way too many people have experienced lately, but it's not forgiveness—you know, forgiving the debt and letting you stay in the house even though you can't pay.

I see what you mean, and that underscores that this theory ends up being a lot less about God's love—including forgiveness—and a lot more about God's demand for justice.

So do you remember earlier how we talked about evaluating these theories on how they reflect the biblical witness, but also in part on how they make us feel or, maybe better, how they help us make sense of God?

Yeah.

Well, I think I've figured some of that out, given what we've just been talking about.

I'd love to hear it.

I think Anselm and company definitely work with some important categories of scripture, particularly those about sin. But I think they're a little too influenced by their medieval context and end up misinterpreting things so that what's most important is sin and God's need to punish it, instead of God's love and God's desire to forgive.

I think that's fair.

And, on the whole, that makes me feel a little nervous about this God. I know I should probably feel relieved that, if I'm a Christian, Jesus has died for me and taken all my punishment. But to be honest, it still leaves me wondering if I can trust this God.

Say more.

If God is so concerned with punishment and justice that God ends up sacrificing God's own child . . . well, I'm just not sure you can trust this God. Ever. It's kind of like maybe you're relieved that your violent dad didn't beat you this time, but what about next time? I don't know, I find the whole picture of this God pretty disturbing.

I think you're right, and you're not alone. I find it pretty disturbing, too.

I like the simplicity and order of Anselm's theory, but I'm not satisfied—no pun intended!—with this theory either, especially because it makes me question the ultimate character of the God we're supposed to worship.

Yeah, like you said, the substitution theory is pretty logical, but it's the cold logic of a business transaction, not the passionate and loving logic of a parent.
There's one other little problem with it as well.

Really—what's that?

At the beginning we talked about how the cross and resurrection go together. That each one only makes sense in light of the other.

Right. I remember. There's obviously no resurrection without the cross. And without the resurrection, Jesus' death is just one more tragedy.

Exactly. Notice, now, that the resurrection plays very little role in the theory put forward by Anselm, Aquinas, and Calvin.

Oh my goodness. You're right. I don't think I would have noticed that, but now that you mention it, it doesn't come into the picture at all.

That's true in Anselm's writing as well. He makes little mention of the resurrection. It's the sign that God has accepted Jesus' payment, and it serves as a symbol and promise about our future fate, but in terms of atonement it's almost superfluous.

That doesn't seem right.

No, it's not.

Okay, so whatever its strengths, this theory also has some issues. So, do you think it would help to go back to our four questions for each theory of atonement?

Sounds good.

Since we've touched on most of this at different points, it should go pretty quickly.

First, what's broken? This is pretty easy to grasp: we've sinned and therefore either offended God's honor in a way we can't make up, or we deserve punishment and death.

Check.

Second, how does God repair this through Jesus? Again, pretty straightforward: Jesus, as the God-man, either more than satisfies God's honor by dying or is punished for us on the cross. Like we said, this all adds up.

Got it.

Third, what does this say about God? Here's where things start to get hairy. God loves us, but God is in a bind because God can't simply forgive us, or even if God sort of forgives us, God needs a mechanism to make that forgiveness happen. No matter how you slice it, it seems like God's sense of honor or justice is just plain more important than God's love. So all the talk about God's love, frankly, rings a little hollow. At the very least, God's love is put in service to God's honor and justice. At the worst, God can't love until justice has been served. Moreover, I'm not sure you can even call it forgiveness if someone has to pay for sin, even if it's the God-man.

Great summary of our issues with this model.

And, fourth, what does this say about our life in the world? I'm not sure what to say. Can you help out with this one?

That depends on which life you mean.

I'm not sure I'm following you.

Well, it has a lot to say about our religious life. As I mentioned, Aquinas modifies Anselm's theory and sets up the whole medieval system of confession and penance that still influences many Christians today. In Calvin, what matters is believing that Jesus was punished for your sins, and so for many Protestants influenced by Calvin the most important thing is *believing* this—that is, actually understanding and agreeing with this theory of atonement.

What about our daily lives? I can see how this shapes our religious practices, but does it say much about our daily lives in the world?

No, not really, or at least not directly. It certainly points to the importance of being a good person and avoiding sin, but it doesn't actually impact our daily lives all that much.

But sometimes I wonder if it has a bigger *indirect* influence on our lives than we realize.

What do you mean?

Well, we mentioned before that the crucifixion can be pretty disturbing because of how violent it is. Like in Mel Gibson's *The Passion of the Christ.*

Yeah, that was disturbing, even pretty grisly.

And that's for a reason. As Anselm's theory continues to be developed, first by Aquinas and Calving but later by other theologians in the United States, there's a greater emphasis on the severity of the punishment Jesus endures. The idea is that as you watch Jesus be tortured and die so horribly, you should feel really, really bad about what you did to make Jesus suffer.

And how does that relate to our lives?

In two ways, I think. First, it kind of signals that violence is okay, at least if it's done according to God's plan. I mean, God achieves atonement through violence, so maybe there are times when we can act in violent ways, too, as long as, you know, we're fighting sin and evil.

Which can be scary, as it seems like there are enough people killing each other in God's name without some theory of atonement backing them up.

And just to be clear, this isn't what Anselm or the others mean, but I wonder if it doesn't tend to glorify violence a bit.

And the second way it influences our lives indirectly?

> I wonder if it doesn't reinforce the idea that the best way to be like Jesus is to suffer the violence of others. After all, that's Jesus' main role, to be punished for someone else.

And you don't think we are to suffer for others.

> There are definitely times when we're called to suffer *for* others and *with* others, but I get worried that this theory of atonement encourages us to imagine that "taking up your cross" is staying in an abusive relationship or suffering oppression.

I think I see what you mean. The whole theory ends up tilting not just toward justice but toward violence and reinforces some pretty unhelpful ways to imagine what it means to be Christian.

> I think so.

That's both interesting and helpful.
But in addition to what it says or doesn't say about our lives, what does it say about *Jesus'* life? I mean, we've said a couple of times that you can't really separate Jesus' life and his cross, but I don't see how this theory stems from the Gospel stories at all.

> You're right. Apart from Jesus being perfect and sinless, what Jesus actually said and did don't matter much at all. Actually, that's not quite true. Jesus serves as an example for us now that we've been forgiven, but it's not like he dies because of anything he said or did; he dies in order to be a sacrifice for us.

I see.

> So, on the whole, what do you think?

Well, I like how seriously it takes our human problem and how neat and logical it all is, but I really don't like the kind of God it assumes. And I don't like the kind of pseudo-forgiveness it promotes. I don't like how disconnected it is from Jesus' life and that it forgets about the resurrection, either.

> So, on the whole, you don't like it.

I guess you could say that.

Any thoughts about why so many people do like it so much? Like I said, it's the most popular game in town right now.

That's a good question. We mentioned earlier that a lot of it probably boils down to just how logical it is. I mean, here we are talking about sin and forgiveness and grace and these four Gospel pictures of the cross and all the rest, and along comes Anselm and company who offer this nice, neat, logical piece of theological work that seems to explain everything. Not only that, but he explains it in a way we're used to, in a way that makes sense. After all, we all operate in the world of accounting sometimes—taking out loans or paying our credit cards and so forth. So I think this theory falls neatly into the world as we know it. It's comfortable, makes sense, and so gives us a sense of control—like we know what's at stake and what we're supposed to do.

I think you're probably right. And, when you put it that way, it sounds fairly persuasive. Are you sure you don't want to stick with this theory of atonement?

Well, I think it's really helpful to know about, especially given how popular it is. But I think I'm looking for a theory that more fully takes into account God's great love for us—that is, it shows that God's love is at least as important as God's justice. We also need a theory that pays attention to the resurrection, and it would be nice if that theory said something more concrete and specific about the lives we actually lead.

Great. Let's go there next.

Insights and Questions

CHAPTER 5

Example and Encouragement

Okay, so we looked at the cross as ransom and victory. And although we liked the idea of God taking our side in the struggles we have, we didn't find that theory completely helpful. It seemed both a little too far out and kind of beneath God to have to bargain with, pay, or trick the devil. Then we looked at the cross as substitute to satisfy God's wrath, and although we appreciated how logical it is, we also felt like that one made God's love a servant to what appears to be a very unloving form of justice. I mean, I know Anselm and company all say that God sends Jesus out of love, but the substitution theory makes it seem like God's holiness or God's justice is way more important than God's love—meaning Jesus has to die before God can really love us.

I think that's a very good summary.

Thanks.
So you said there's a third way of looking at atonement we should look at?

Yeah, although it's really more than just one way or theory. It's more like a school of ways of looking at the cross. Just like there's more than one way to look at the cross as God's ransom, and just like a number of theologians work in slightly different ways on the idea of the cross as substitute, this third school represents a variety of theologians who aren't satisfied with either the ransom or substitutionary models of atonement.

All right. So where do we begin with this one?

Right where we left off with the shortcomings of the substitutionary theory. Because even though Anselm's theory was very popular, there were people right from the beginning who felt that God's love gets seriously underemphasized.

So these theologians want to make the atonement about God's love?

Yes, and about the power of God's love to transform us into loving people. This actually is a big emphasis in the New Testament. In one letter, in fact, the author comes right out and says, "God is love" (1 John 4:8). And this theme appears in lots of the writings of early Christian theologians, as well, but it's given new and dynamic shape in response to the popularity of Anselm by a man named Peter Abelard.

Did he know Anselm?

Probably not personally, although he was familiar with Anselm's work. Abelard was born about fifty years after Anselm and started his career as a philosopher, teacher, theologian, and monk while Anselm was still working.

And I gather Abelard wasn't too crazy about what Anselm did with the cross.

No, he wasn't. In particular, he didn't think Anselm's satisfaction theory was ultimately all that different than the ransom theory of atonement.

Really? I thought Anselm's theory was almost the opposite of the ransom theory.

On one level, it is—God doesn't need to negotiate with, let alone pay or trick, the devil. This isn't about God or humanity owing something to the devil, but instead is about what is owed to God.

Which sounds like the opposite.

At another level, though, and as we mentioned briefly, both systems are about payment. In the older scheme, the devil demands payment, and that's what Jesus offers with his death on the cross. In Anselm's later scheme, God demands payment—satisfaction for God's offended honor or violated justice—and, again, that's what Jesus offers with his death on the cross.

Ah, right. I remember now. Both theories are essentially accounting systems. That's easier to see with Anselm's theory, but the earlier view is also about debits and credits; it's just the devil who demands payment, not God.

Right. Abelard rejected the whole notion of payment when it comes to our relationship with God, whether it's to the devil or to God. Further, he questioned how one sin can fix another.

I'm not sure I'm following.

Anselm's theory turns on the redemptive power of Jesus' substitutionary sacrifice. But for that sacrifice to happen, people had to kill Jesus. So Abelard wondered how humanity could be saved by committing the sin of crucifying Jesus. In fact, he looked back to the story of Adam and Eve and asked how eating an apple, even if it's against God's command, could possibly be worse than killing the Son of God. In short, he wasn't sure why Jesus' death—especially considering the fact that we humans put Jesus to death—could possibly count for us and not against us.

So Abelard was essentially asking Anselm how it is that two wrongs make a right.

Exactly. His pushing the accounting system inherent in Anselm's theory to its logical conclusion doesn't seem, if you're pardon the pun, to add up.

So what did Abelard propose instead?

He went back to some of the earliest Christian writings—both in the New Testament itself as well as in some of the works of early Christian theologians—and was convinced that Anselm and others miss two huge things. The first, as we mentioned, is God's love and, as we'll see, the power of God's love to shape us into beings worthy of God's

love. The second thing Abelard drew attention to is how *all* of Jesus'
life, not just his death, is about love.

**You know, that's interesting. Each of the first two theories focused almost
entirely on the single event of the cross. Neither one seemed particularly
interested in the rest of Jesus' life, almost as if it doesn't really matter.**

That's right. What mattered in each of the first two is the cross. Not
what came before it. Not what led up to it. Not even the particular
details of it.

What do you mean, not even the details of it?

Earlier we paid attention to the different emphases of the four Gospel
writers when they describe the cross.

**And about how you can learn a lot about how each Gospel writer understands
Jesus through some of the differences between the Gospels. And how, taken
together, these differences offer us a deeper, even truer, picture of Jesus.**

Right. But in the first two theories none of those details—about Jesus'
life or about his death—really matter. It's like what the first two theories are really focused on is a larger system, essentially a cosmic
accounting system, and in particular on how Jesus' death counts as
a huge payment in that system to deal with the problem of human
sin.

So they're not all that interested in *how* Jesus died but more *that* he died.

Well put. It matters, especially in the substitutionary theory that Calvin and his later followers developed, that it was a horrible death so
we understand the depth of our sin that he was punished for. But
otherwise what matters, as you said, is *that* he died and that his death
counts for payment—either as ransom to the devil or as satisfaction
to God.

**And that seems to be even truer of Jesus' life, as these theories don't seem to
pay any particular attention to his life and teaching, almost as if they don't
really matter at all.**

Exactly, and this is what Abelard and later folks in this school want to
go back to. They want to show us how all of Jesus' life demonstrates

God's love and serves as a divine example and encouragement.

Example and encouragement—as opposed to ransom and victory or substitution and satisfaction.

Right. First and foremost, Jesus—his life, teaching, and death—are all an example of God's love in two important ways.

Can you explain that a bit more?

Sure. First, they're an example of how much God loves us. Like Anselm and others, Abelard wants to say that God sends Jesus to us because God loves us.

I guess for this one, you don't have to look much further than the world's most famous Bible verse, John 3:16: "For God so loved the world that he gave his only Son . . ."

That's right. And what's more, God not only sends Jesus out of love, but Jesus also teaches us again and again about just how much God loves us. Think of his parable of the prodigal son. In the story, the younger son (the prodigal son) runs off and wastes his inheritance.

But when he returns home a mess, his father embraces him and throws him a party. He still loves his son. Jesus teaches us that God is, first and foremost, not just about love in general but is actually in love with all of us.

So Jesus' primary job and purpose is to teach us about God's love.

Right, although not just through his teaching but also his life. I mean, he actually goes and dies for us out of love. In John's Gospel, as we mentioned earlier, Jesus talks about himself as the Good Shepherd, the one who lays down his life for the sheep (10:17). Later, Jesus says that there is no greater love than to lay down your life for another (15:13). And this is exactly what Jesus does for us.

So for Abelard and company, the cross is primarily an expression of God's great love. The key here is that it's not a ransom or a trick. It's not a way of paying an offended or angry God. It's about Jesus showing us God's love.

Right. And it's not something new. It's the culmination of all of Jesus' life and ministry up to this point.

You said that Jesus gives us examples of love in two ways. What's the second?

The second is that in addition to showing us that *God loves us*, Jesus also shows us how *we ought to love each other*. After all, Jesus doesn't only say that he loves us and proves it by dying for us, he also says, "I give you a new commandment, that you love one another. Just as I have loved you, you also should love one another. By this everyone will know that you are my disciples, if you have love for one another" (John 13:34-35).

Interesting. So Jesus' life and death are examples of how we should live, too.

Exactly. Jesus teaches us that we should love, and he also teaches us *how* to love through stories like the Good Samaritan, where the religious outcast, a Samaritan, takes care of a man who's been beaten by robbers (Luke 10:25-37).

And then there's Jesus' teaching about "turning the other cheek."

Right. In fact, many of the Gospel stories about Jesus are about how we should treat each other.

That actually makes a lot of sense. And it's a whole lot like what I, and I think most people, think Christianity is all about—taking care of others, being better people, and so on. But I'm not sure I understand how this relates to atonement. We said earlier that atonement ultimately is just what it says: *at-one-ment*, taking something that is broken and repairing it. So how does this fix what's broken? Or, for that matter, what *is* broken according to Abelard?

What do you mean?

Well, in the first two theories we looked at, the problem—what's broken—was pretty clear. In the first version, it's that humanity has sinned and is therefore captive to the devil. And that leads to how atonement works—Jesus' death is payment or ransom to the devil, and through that God releases humanity. And everything is fixed. Whatever problems we might have with this theory, at least the problem and solution are clearly stated.

Same with the second theory.

Right. With the second one, the problem is that through our sin we've offended God's honor or justice, and so the demand for honor or justice needs to be satisfied, and Jesus' death does that. Again, a clear statement of the problem and solution.

And you don't see a parallel in Abelard.

Not really. I like his emphasis on love, but I can't quite tell what he thinks is broken, let alone how he thinks Jesus' life and death fix things.

That's a great observation. Maybe it's that Abelard doesn't think things are quite as broken as earlier theologians did.

What do you mean?

For Abelard, all of life is about love. All of it. Anselm was all about holiness, and Calvin was all about justice; here it's all about love. God is love, God loves us, we are to love each other, and so forth. So the problem is that love is at the center of absolutely everything in life, and yet we humans don't really know how to love each other.

So Jesus came to teach us.

Yes, but it's more than that, because even when we're given a good example, we can't follow it.

Say a little more.

Sure. There are, essentially, two interrelated problems: First, we don't seem to know how to love. So Jesus comes and gives us great examples of how to love each other.

But Jesus, it seems, isn't the only one to do that. The Old Testament prophets do that, don't they? Philosophers like Socrates might do that. And people like Gandhi and Mother Teresa and Martin Luther King Jr., and all kinds of other good people can do that, too. Right? I mean, even if you don't think they give perfect examples of how to live, like Jesus does, you'd still have to admit that there are lots of good examples of love all around us.

I think you're right. Often the most powerful examples are found right in our own families and among friends and neighbors.

So why does Jesus' example become so important?

First, as you said, Jesus' example is of perfect love. But, more importantly, Jesus' example doesn't just *teach* us how to love; it also touches us so deeply in our hearts and minds that it *moves* us to actually love others in a more profound and godly way. In a sense, Jesus is both example and encouragement, even inspiration.

I'm not sure I'm following.

Jesus' whole life teaches us two things: first, that God loves us; second, that we should love others. Further, he shows us what that kind of love looks like. Finally, he actually demonstrates perfect love by dying for us. And when we see how much he loves us—how much God loves us—we are actually transformed, changed, moved to love others like Jesus loves us.

Okay, I think I'm beginning to see what you mean. In terms of the problem, it's that we were made to love each other, but we don't. The solution, then, is that God sends Jesus to teach us how to love and to encourage and inspire us, even transform us, to do so.

Right.

But is that enough to fix things? I mean, does that really mend whatever is broken between God and us?

Again, that's a great question. For Abelard and those who follow him, there isn't quite the same sense of brokenness, of hopelessness, that colors the other theories. In the ransom theory, things are hopeless because we've become captive to the devil and there's absolutely nothing we can do to escape that. In the substitution theory, it's hopeless because we owe God complete obedience and honor, but we've totally wrecked that through our sin and so deserve punishment, and, again, there's absolutely no way we can escape that condition. With Abelard, though, the problem is that because God is perfect love and we often fail to love others, we can't live with God eternally. However, if we learn to love and are inspired to love, then we *can* live with God.

So this theory isn't about forgiveness, then? What did Abelard make of all the talk about forgiveness of sin in the Bible? That seems like something that Anselm took pretty seriously.

Abelard would probably say that in one sense it's *all* about forgiveness of sin. After all, Jesus doesn't wait until after the cross to start forgiving people. He forgives people all over the place. That's part of what gets him into trouble—he dares to forgive just about anybody. In fact, he goes so far as to say that there is more rejoicing in heaven over one sinner who repents than over ninety-nine righteous people (Luke 15:7).

So Abelard didn't think the cross was necessary in order for God to forgive?

That's exactly what he said. In fact, Abelard would argue that New Testament stories about Jesus suggest that, more often than not, God is way more ready, and even eager, to forgive than we are to receive forgiveness.

So the cross doesn't make forgiveness possible; it shows us that God loves us enough to always forgive us.

Exactly. After all, not only does Jesus go around forgiving everyone during his ministry, but even from the cross he prays, "Father, forgive them; for they do not know what they are doing" (Luke 23:34).

But how does this make it possible for us to love perfectly, or at least better? Isn't that what Abelard was saying the cross is all about?

The whole of Jesus' life, actually, is meant to teach us about love and inspire us to love others, but, yes, in the cross we are confronted with such a profound picture of love that we will be inspired, even transformed, to love others. And as we learn to love others, we also become more lovable, more deserving of God's love, and thereby able to live with God.

So that's atonement for Abelard? Being transformed by God's love into more loving, more lovable people?

Pretty much.
 So what do you think?

I like it. I like it a lot, actually. I mean, when I think about all the experiences I've had in my life, I can probably say that the experiences of being loved, really loved, by someone—those really are the most powerful experiences I've had. Same with loving someone else. Love is just plain powerful.

I agree with you. Love is pretty incredible. And that's the real strength of Abelard's theory. It takes what seems to be mostly missing, or at least in the background of the other theories, and puts it right up front.

Where it ought to be, I think.
At the same time, though . . .

Yes?

Well, I'm not sure how to put this, but as much as I like Abelard's emphasis on love, I'm just not sure it does the trick. Or at least it doesn't quite seem to cover the bases, if you know what I mean.

Say a little more.

Well, let's go back to the questions we've been asking about each of the models we've been looking at.

Okay.

What's the problem? What's broken? Easy. We don't know how to love, and we're not capable of loving.

Got it.

And what's the solution? Jesus teaches us how to love and inspires us, even transforms us, to be able to love by showing us how much God loves us. Right?

Right. And the third question, about God?

This is where it gets interesting. What does it tell us about God? That God is all loving. That God's chief characteristic is love. That God is, finally, all about love, just like the Bible says. I like that part a lot.

I do, too.
So what about the Christian life? What does this model have to offer here?

This is where this Abelard really shines. I mean, break out your bracelets—WWJD, What Would Jesus Do? The loving thing, of course, and because Jesus has given us all kinds of examples all over Scripture, we can look to him to get it right. In some ways, this is the first theory of atonement to take either Jesus' life or ours seriously. And I think that's important.

You don't sound totally convinced, though.

No I'm not. I like it a lot, but I'm just not sure Abelard told the whole story, or maybe he didn't take our human story seriously enough.

What do you mean?

Well, it seems like Abelard thought, as we've said, that the major problem is that we don't know how to love and can't love. Again, I think there's something powerfully true about this. But that seems to reduce everything essentially to a lack of education. We don't know enough, so Jesus shows us.

And maybe a lack of motivation, too.

That's fair. Okay, a lack of education and motivation. But doesn't that suddenly sound a lot like school, or maybe school sports? I mean, isn't that what a good teacher or coach does—teaches and inspires you? Is that really what we think Jesus is—a super teacher and coach? Don't get me wrong; I've had some awesome teachers and coaches. I'm just wondering if this is really what Jesus is.

I think I see what you mean.

Further, why do we need Jesus? Don't we already have great examples of how to love in the Old Testament? Aren't all those laws essentially supposed to teach us about what we should do for others? And doesn't the Old Testament also stress how much God loves us? So what's the point of Jesus?

Those are very good questions. So why do you think Jesus comes?

I'm not sure. I guess that's what I'm uncomfortable with. It seems like Abelard understood Jesus mostly in terms of helping us be better people. Again, I'm all for that. I'm just not sure why we need Jesus to show us.

I think Abelard and others from this school of thought would say that we do, in fact, have lots of great examples of what God wants us to do in the Old Testament. But there's something about the Son of God coming to teach us that makes it all hit home.

But does he have to die? I mean, that's a pretty expensive lesson.

Abelard would say, I think, that nothing less than the cross displays so powerfully the transformative love of God.

Maybe. I don't know, though.

You're actually not alone in wondering about this.

Well, I'm guessing folks who prefer the substitutionary theory of atonement don't like Abelard at all.

You're absolutely right. But I meant that even some of those who follow Abelard have raised some of the same questions. Are Jesus' life and death really only about moral improvement? And does this explain why Jesus had to die?

So what did they say?

All kinds of things, actually. But most of it can be boiled down to saying that Jesus' life and death not only teach us about love and inspire us to love, they also create a new community of people who have been transformed—and are still being transformed—by God's love. This view became very popular in the nineteenth century and is still pretty popular today.

It sounds interesting, but could you say a little more?

Sure. One of the things that Jesus talks about a lot—in fact, in Matthew, Mark, and Luke it's the thing Jesus seems to talk the most about—is the kingdom of God. Later followers of Abelard think that Jesus' preaching and teaching about God's love was really preaching and teaching about the kind of community God wanted and was going to create.

I'm not sure I'm following.

Well, one way to read the Genesis story of the fall of Adam and Eve is to see it as the disintegration of trust. The serpent introduces mistrust into a previously trusting and harmonious relationship between God and Adam and Eve. And once Adam and Eve don't trust God, they disobey God. From the beginning, though, what God wants from humanity is a trusting, loving relationship. The Ten Commandments lay out the parameters of what that kind of community would look like, and the prophets regularly call God's people back to that kind of community, but it never really succeeds.

So, God gets involved more directly, in the person of Jesus. And through his teaching about the kingdom of God and through his ministry of healing and feeding and helping and all the other stuff he does, Jesus again shows us what this kind of community looks like. Then, he's killed—in large part because he preaches that God really is all about love, and really does want this kind of loving community. Through his death, Jesus creates a new community and makes it possible for us to enter into a new relationship with God and with each other.

That actually sounds pretty good. But how? How does his death do that?

It's a little hard to pin down, even in its modern form, but essentially proponents of this theory suggest that the followers of Jesus are made into a new community, even a new humanity, by the power of the Holy Spirit. In some ways, this view of atonement embodies Luke's vision of all these different people—men and women, young and old, Jews and Gentiles, slaves and free—joined together in Christ.

Sounds almost like the motto on our coins: *E Pluribus Unum*, "Out of the many, one."

You're right, but it's a community joined not only politically or nationally, but ethically as well, bound to each other in love to care for each other, share with each other, see each other differently, as God sees us.

Are you, by chance, familiar with the rock and roll band, U2?

Familiar? I've got all their albums and have been to half a dozen concerts!

Cool. Then you're familiar with their song "One."

Absolutely.

Think of some of the repeating elements from "One" as summing up this view of the new community in Christ.

**"One love / one life / when it's one need / in the night."
I think I get it.**

Right, and then the refrain. . .

"We're one, but we're not the same. / We get to / carry each other / carry each other. / One."

Yeah, that's beginning to make sense. And quite beautiful.

But?

Well, I guess it's at this point that I should admit that I grew up in Missouri.

Sorry, but I think you just totally lost me.

I'm just kidding. Missouri is the "Show me" state. I didn't grow up there, but I might as well have, because I'd like to see a few examples of this new community of people inspired by Jesus to be perfectly loving.

Again, don't get me wrong. It's not that I don't think love is the ticket; I also agree that Christians should model a new kind of community, one that's based on love. But, to be perfectly honest, it's not what I see. I mean, I know there are some great congregations and some really great people at church. But let's face it, Christian's have done a lot of harm throughout history, too. Just think of the Crusades, or the Inquisition, or the Christians who opposed civil rights, or some of the hateful rhetoric you hear today.

You're absolutely right. Christians have often not lived up to the kind of new community and kingdom of God that Jesus proclaimed.

Again, I think there have been lots of great Christians, from St. Francis to Martin Luther King Jr. to Mother Teresa; and lots of great churches; and lots of great things Christians have done, from starting hospitals to caring for the poor, and so on. But, let's be honest, not only are Christians not perfect, but people from many other faith communities do wonderful things, too. Gandhi, the Dalai Lama, Eli Wiesel, and others—they have done wonderful things, and many of them don't even believe in Jesus or the significance of his death. So . . . I guess I'm back to my original question: where is this new community, and how does Jesus' death create it?

Great question. Essentially, you're saying that, sure, Jesus' life, ministry, and death set a great example, but where's the payoff? Where's the actual and unique difference it makes that you can see—not in the lives of a few people, but in the larger Christian community and world?

Right. In the end it seems like in this theory it's all up to us. Jesus sets the example, but we have to follow it. And I guess I'm just not confident that we can.

I see what you mean.

And I'm not just talking about other people. I also have a hard time acting in a loving way, even to people I really do love and who I know love me.

Me too.

So maybe this theory just doesn't take human sinfulness, human brokenness and need seriously enough. That's kind of the picture Abelard seems to paint of humanity, isn't it? That we just need a little more instruction and some good inspiration and we'll be okay.

There's no question that this model of atonement has a more optimistic view of human capabilities than the other two. For this reason it focuses very much on our moral life because it has confidence that we can, indeed, make significant ethical change in our lives. In fact, some call it the "moral influence" theory for just that reason.

And that's great. But focusing on our behavior doesn't seem to be quite enough. It's like I don't just need a new instruction manual; I need a new heart, too, a new desire to really do what I've been taught.

I think Abelard would say that, ultimately, that's what the cross achieves: it actually creates in us new hearts. We see in Jesus God's gift of love poured out for us and the whole world, and it makes a genuine difference. It makes it possible for us to be more loving.

And I appreciate that, really. This theory, more than any other so far, has something concrete and helpful to say about the actual shape of our Christian lives in the world. But when it comes to actually making those lives happen, I just don't think it works. It doesn't seem to go deep enough or really change things. I know it's supposed to transform us, but somehow Jesus' cross, I think, needs to be about more than our behavior. The cross needs to be about everything.

Which reminds me of something, now that I think of it.

What's that?

Where's the resurrection?

What?

The resurrection. Where is it in Abelard's theory? Why does it matter? Does it matter? Just like with Anselm, I haven't heard any talk about the resurrection from Abelard, either; only about Jesus' life and death as examples of God's love for us and of how we should love others.

That's a very good point. There's not much trace of the resurrection in Abelard's work, at least as it relates to atonement.

What about later Christians who developed Abelard's thought? Do they have anything to say about the resurrection?

To be honest, not a whole lot. The resurrection represents the triumph of God's love—Jesus who loved perfectly is not lost to death but is raised to new life. In this way, the resurrected Jesus continues to function as an example and promise of what we might become, too.

If we work hard enough, or improve enough, or are inspired enough, or even accept that we've been transformed enough. I don't know; it just feels a bit like window dressing to me.

What do you mean?

Just that, again, the resurrection doesn't seem particularly necessary. Kind of like an afterthought. And, really, that makes some sense. If the emphasis is on Jesus as example, then you're kind of done when he dies.

It sounds like, on the whole, you're not satisfied with this theory either.

Well, this way of understanding the cross definitely has some real strengths. I just wish I could believe it.

What do you mean?

Well, we've said that we'll assess these different theories on how they reflect what the Bible says—which this one does pretty well—and how the theories affect us. Do they ring true to us or help us explain life? And, well, I guess this one does give me good examples and inspires me, but it doesn't convince me. I just don't think I can do it. I need more than a good example. I need someone who can honestly save us, transform us, and make a difference.

That's a pretty fair assessment.

So where do we go from here? Three up, three down. If this were baseball, the inning would be over. Are there any more models to consider?

I'm sure there are, though these three—ransom and victory, satisfaction and substitution, and example and encouragement—really do represent the best of Christian thinking about the atonement.

Uh oh. I've learned a ton about the cross so far, and I appreciate that, because I can see how each of these theories may help me at different times of my life. But I'm still not sure I really understand the cross. I feel like we've been thinking and thinking ourselves around in circles, but I'm not sure, finally, that I *get* it—why Jesus had to die and what difference that makes.

But maybe that's the problem.

What do you mean?

Maybe we've been *thinking* about the cross instead of just *experiencing* it. Maybe we've reduced atonement to an idea instead of realizing it's an *action*, an *experience*. Maybe we need to stop with all the theories and models and instead go back to look again at what God is actually doing in and through the cross and resurrection of Jesus.

I'm not sure I'm following, but I'll give it a try.

Good. Then let's go there next.

Insights and Questions

CHAPTER 6

Event and Experience

At this point, I think I would benefit from a bit of a recap.

Why don't you try to summarize things.

I had a feeling you were going to say that.

Seriously, though, you've done that very well at a number of points, and I'm sure you can pull it together now.

Okay, here we go.

We've looked at three ideas—or, really, three groups of ideas—models or theories about how to understand and make sense of the cross. They're pretty different. Each has some real strengths, and each some real limitations.

The first theory understands the cross in terms of ransom and victory. Its strength is that it emphasizes the resurrection and takes seriously God's struggle to rescue us from death and the devil and all the things that oppress us. Its shortcoming is the whole idea that we're somehow captive to the devil and that God has to pay or trick the devil into letting us go. Even if you believe in a devil, it's hard to understand why God has to treat the devil like an equal. The whole theory just feels a little closer to *Star Wars* than it does everyday life.

I think that captures the first theory well.

Thanks.

The second theory rejects the idea that God has to pay off the devil and instead imagines our condition as being similar to that of a peasant who has offended the honor of the king. Because we owe God all honor, there's no way once we've sinned that we could ever make our offense up to God. In a sense, we've incurred this huge debt to God and can't pay it. So we deserve to die, or worse, to go to hell. Which means God is in something of a bind. God loves us and wants to save us, but at the same time, God—as God—can't just forgive us; that would violate God's honor and justice. So God sends Jesus. As someone who is truly human, yet without ever sinning, Jesus can stand in our place, giving God the honor that God deserves in one theory, and taking our punishment for us in another. Either way, as someone who is truly God, what Jesus does for us has extraordinary significance; it ends up counting for all of us.

> So to get back to the accounting analogy you mentioned . . . Because Jesus is God, Jesus is able to pay the debt for us; and because Jesus is human, what he pays counts for all of us.

Right. And that points to the main strength of this theory: it's logical. It makes sense—everything adds up, both literally and figuratively.

But the problem is that it's kind of a cold logic—it's all about debts and payments and honor and justice. Before long, God ends up looking more like a demanding Ebenezer Scrooge kind of accountant than a loving parent. I guess, on the whole, it's just too easy to read a couple of Bible verses through the lens of medieval feudalism and end up losing sight of anything about God's love. I mean, God sends Jesus out of love, but on the whole, the dominant thing about this theory seems to be God's justice, God's anger, and God's righteous need for punishment. Someone needs to be punished—blood needs to be shed—before God is willing to act in a loving way toward us. More than that, it's hard to understand why we call it forgiveness when Jesus pays the debt for us. All the talk about the forgiveness of sins ends up ringing a little hollow. Finally, not only does the resurrection seem kind of unnecessary, but this theory doesn't really connect to Jesus' life and ministry in any meaningful way or say that much about the shape of our lives in the world.

So, ultimately this theory doesn't seem satisfying theologically or true to the whole of the biblical witness and its emphasis on God's love.

Right. And that brings us to the third theory, which seems *all* about God's love. Through his life, teaching, and ministry, Jesus shows us how much God loves us and shows us that we ought to love each other. More than that, Jesus also shows us *how* to love each other, especially in his teaching. But the cross is God's ultimate expression of love. That's where Jesus gives his life for us, and that—at least in theory—should inspire us to love others as God has loved us.

So the emphasis on God's love is great. And it's cool that this theory takes into account Jesus' whole life, rather than just the cross. What's more, this is probably the first theory of atonement that has much to say about our actual daily lives as Christians, namely, that we should follow the example Jesus set.

But the problem is that if Jesus' death is mainly an example, it doesn't seem to have worked. And if it's supposed to transform us—make us into a new community—well, even though it's a beautiful idea, it seems to promise more than it can deliver. I mean, there just aren't too many of us who follow his example, and it doesn't really explain very convincingly how Jesus' example helps restore our broken relationship with God. And, once again, the resurrection seems like an afterthought.

Wow—another great summary.

Thanks.

So where do we go from here? You said earlier that you thought these three theories represent much of the best of what Christians have said to explain the cross.

Yeah, I've been thinking about that. About how all of the theories have something valuable in them but none of them seems, ultimately, to do the trick. And I wondered if maybe the problem is that, in fact, they're *theories*. Each one of them gets caught up in *explaining* the cross instead of helping us *experience* it.

I was interested when you said that a little earlier, but I'm not totally sure what you mean.

I'm not sure I've worked it out completely either, so we may need to figure it out together.

I'm game.

Great.

Okay, so it struck me that when we talked about each of the theories we ended up trying to fit the cross into some larger framework about humanity's problem—namely, how our relationship with God has been damaged. After all, that's what atonement—as *at-one-ment*—is all about: fixing something that's broken. And so each of the theories starts by explaining what the problem is.

With the first theory, it's that we're captive to devil and death and can't free ourselves; in the second, it's that we've offended God's honor and justice by sinning and can't make it up on our own, so we deserve punishment; and in the third, it's that we're not loving enough and so can't live in relationship with the all-loving God.

Right. And then with that picture of what's broken, each theory explains how Jesus and his cross fix things.

In the first theory, Jesus is given as ransom or is taken by death and the devil, but he is too great to be contained and thereby rescues us. In the second, he pays our debt or is punished for us. And in the third, he teaches us how to love and transforms and inspires us actually to love others.

Right again.

So what's the problem? I mean, I know that each of these theories has its own distinct shortcomings. That's why we're still talking about all this. But what's the problem with starting with what's broken and then describing how Jesus fixes things?

Well, I guess there's nothing wrong with it *in theory*, except that's exactly the problem in the first place.

Sorry, you lost me with that one.

Well, each of these *theories* about us and God and atonement and all are useful. But we don't live theoretically; we actually live. We aren't in a theoretical relationship with God; we're in an actual relationship. We aren't broken in theory; we're actually broken. We don't need to be fixed or healed or redeemed—or however you want to describe it—in theory; we need to be actually healed and restored. I think the problem with theories—and models, too, for that matter—is that we can look at them, discuss them, and evaluate them, but all the while never really be touched by them.

I think I'm beginning to catch on, but can you say a little more?

Let's try a few examples.

Always a great idea.

Okay, so let's say you're going on a date. There are all kinds of magazine articles and books about dating with all kinds of theories about how to find the right person, about what a good date should be like, about how to make the most out of your date. But none of those is like being on a date. None of them can really prepare you for, let alone substitute for, actually going out with someone.

No kidding!

It's the same with parenting. Again, you can read all kinds of articles and books, or watch television programs that give advice and offer various parenting models. But none of them actually makes you a parent. Don't get me wrong. I've read some great books on parenting that have really helped. But ultimately you become a parent by parenting.

So you're saying that these theories of atonement end up being just that—theories?

Yeah, I think that's what I'm saying.

But isn't that okay? I mean, isn't that what theories do—explain things? What is it you want them to do?

That's a great question. I don't think you can escape some level of theory, of explanation. It's what helps us talk about all kinds of things, including the cross. But somehow it feels like the cross gets lost in the theory.

What do you mean?

Each of the theories we've looked at makes the cross fit into a larger scheme, or plan, about how atonement happens. And, like we said, I can understand why that's appealing, even helpful. But when you're done, it feels like the cross is just some cog in a larger "atonement machine." It's a means to an end, not an end or event itself.

An event?

Yes, an event. For instance, think back to the four Gospel stories we looked at about the cross. In the Gospels, there's no avoiding the cross. It's not part of some larger plan; it's just the cross—this big, scary, messy, frightening, tragic event.

So are you saying that in each of the theories it's like the cross serves some larger purpose, and that almost makes it a *good* thing? Maybe not nice to look at, but ultimately a good thing.

Right. Like it's all part of God's plan, God's grand design.

And you don't think it is?

I think I used to. And I'm not sure I want to say it's *not* part of any plan, or that God doesn't have any plan. At the same time, though, I think there are a couple of problems in making the cross just some part of a much larger plan.

For instance?

Well, first, and like we've said before, none of these "plans" totally makes sense. In the first theory, why does God have to ransom or rescue us from the devil? Come on—it's God we're talking about after all.

I think I see where you're going. In the second theory, we had all kinds of questions, too. For instance, how is this really forgiveness if Jesus has to pay God a debt or be punished for us? Like we said, it feels like more of an accounting scheme than anything else.

Right; and we found the same thing with the third theory: why does witnessing Jesus' death on the cross make us more loving? Even more, it apparently doesn't work. Most of us, if we're honest, aren't like Jesus.

So part of what you're saying is that if the cross is just some part of God's larger plan, then it seems like none of the plans actually works that well. I mean, when you push them, they don't hold together; they don't totally make sense.

Yes, I think that's where I've ended up.

But it sounds like something more, like there's something bigger at stake for you as well.

I think you're right. I think I get worried that when we reduce the events of Jesus' life, death, and resurrection to a part of some larger plan, they lose their impact on us. I mean, we might figure every-thing out theoretically, but we're not actually any different.

That reminds me of what we said earlier—that we need to assess these differ-ent theories by paying attention to how they connect to what the Bible says about the cross *and* to the difference they make to our lives in this world. But with each of the three we've looked at, it sounds like at the end of the day we're still the same old people, just armed with a plan that explains how it's all okay.

Exactly! And that's just not what the biblical witness seems to talk about when it talks about Jesus' cross.

What do you mean?

> Let's go back to the Gospel accounts again. In all of them, as we noticed earlier, no one believes what happened at first. They seem totally unprepared for Jesus' actual death, like they just can't believe he was really crucified, even though he told them it was coming. And they don't believe the resurrection at first, either.

But when they do, it changes everything.

> Right; it changes *everything*. Thomas confesses that Jesus is not just his Lord, but God (John 20:27-29), and all the disciples go out to proclaim what God has done through Jesus' cross and resurrection. Christian tradition says, in fact, that most of the disciples themselves are eventually put to death for their faith.

I think I see what you mean. It's hard to imagine dying for a plan, whether it's a supernatural plan like the ransom theory, a cold and calculating plan like the substitutionary theory, or a lovely but inadequate plan like Abelard's theory of Jesus as a divine example.

> Plans, models, and theories don't change people. We see that in the Gospels, but we see it in the writings of the apostle Paul, too. Paul actually calls the cross an offense, a stumbling block.

Something that gets in the way, something that actually affects you, even messes with you and your world.

> Yes; and all the talk about theories and plans seems to remove, or at least disguise, the offense that Paul is talking about. So I'm wondering now if the problem with the three theories we've been discussing is that it seems like it ends there. The theories *explain* the cross to us, but they don't *do* the cross to us. They *explain* how atonement happens, but they don't *make* atonement happen for us.

I'm not sure what you mean by "doing" the cross or "making atonement happen."

> Like I said, I'm not sure I've got this all figured out, either. But I think that it's a real problem that you can listen to all of these theories and not be any different when you're done.

Say a little more.

Maybe it will help to go back once again to the Gospel stories about the cross.

Okay.

Actually, we should probably look at the whole biblical story before moving to the cross.

Are you really sure we have that much time?!

I was actually thinking of just a one- or two-sentence summary.

Whew!
Okay, I'm ready.

Here goes, then.

In some ways, the whole of the Old Testament could be summarized as the story of God's love poured out for the world. It begins with creation but continues as God's wayward creatures turn away from God's love. Like a faithful parent, God won't give up. And so God comes after us in covenants and laws, and through the prophets who speak messages of both judgment and promise. Through it all, God is trying to restore and redeem us.

Kind of like the whole Bible is about atonement.

Right; at least after chapter 3 in Genesis.

Chapter 3?

The first two chapters of Genesis tell the story of creation in two different ways. Chapter 3 continues the second story by describing what's often called "the fall," the story of Adam and Eve and the temptation to turn away from God.

I remember we talked about that earlier and, if memory serves, they totally give in to the temptation.

They do, just as we all have ever since.

And so the story of the Old Testament is about God trying to get us back? That makes sense. But what about the New Testament? I mean, if the Old

Testament is, in a sense, all about atonement, what makes the New Testament any different?

> That's a great question. In some ways the New Testament continues the story of God's love and God's desire to redeem us, to make us all one again. If there's a difference, it's probably that in the New Testament it gets way more personal for God.

What do you mean? I thought the stories in the Old Testament portray God as pretty passionate.

> Absolutely. God is totally and fully committed to humanity, and God's passion for us and creation oozes out on almost every page of the Old Testament. What I meant was that in the New Testament, we see God entering the story more directly, more personally, in and through Jesus. In fact, the New Testament confesses that Jesus is the Word of God made flesh (John 1:1, 14).

Incarnation, if I remember correctly.

> Yes, exactly. See? You are becoming a theologian.

Now that's scary!

But seriously, are you saying that in the New Testament God gets involved in the story in a firsthand kind of way by entering into the creation directly through Jesus?

> Right. Again, God is very involved in the Old Testament, too, but God enters into not just the story but our actual existence, the human condition itself, by taking on our flesh.

And so what difference does that make?

> Here's where it's important to go back to the biblical story, not just about the cross but about Jesus' life and ministry and everything that leads up to the cross.

That sounds like a big topic, too, so I feel another summary coming on.

> Here it is: Jesus bears God's presence and love to the world by preaching the coming kingdom of God, teaching people to love each other, doing miracles to feed and heal people, and forgiving people their sins.

That sounds like the Bible stories I heard in Sunday school, all right.

Except I left one part out.

Yes?

And the people kill him for it.

Wait. I don't quite understand. I know Jesus dies, but are you saying people killed Jesus *because* of these things? I mean, I've heard some bad sermons and lectures before, but I don't think I'd kill someone for that. And as for healing, feeding, and forgiving—doesn't everyone want that?

Well, definitely the feeding and healing part.

What's wrong with forgiveness? Don't most people want that, too?

Good point. Okay, I forgive you.

Wait a second, what did I ever do to you?!

What does it matter? Didn't you just say that most people want forgiveness? I figured you were like most people, so I forgave you.

Yeah, but come on, I didn't do anything.

So?

So? Well, if I didn't do anything, than who are you to forgive me?

Exactly.

Ah . . . I think I see what you mean. Forgiveness is great if you want it, if you know you did something wrong. But if you don't think you've done anything wrong, it's a huge bummer and actually kind of offensive, like you're accusing me of something.

Right.

It's weird, because when we talk about forgiveness, we always assume it's a good thing, something really nice. But when you suddenly forgave me, it actually made me kind of mad. Like I couldn't believe you had the nerve to forgive me when I hadn't done anything.

Because forgiveness always implies judgment.

Which reminds me of something former first lady Pat Nixon once said.

Really?

Yeah. She said that the day Gerald Ford pardoned her husband was the hardest day of her life. I never really understood that, because most people thought that if Ford hadn't pardoned Nixon there probably would have been a trial, and he might have gone to jail. But if she didn't think he'd done anything wrong, then it would have been deeply offensive to hear Ford offer a pardon—essentially, forgiveness—to her husband.

I think that's exactly right.

Is this what Paul means when he says the cross is an offense?

I think that's part of it. For both Jews and Romans of Paul's day, crucifixion was the worst punishment available. Partly because of how painful it is—so painful, in fact, that Roman citizens could not be crucified. But it's also because of the social stigma crucifixion carried. It was, in many ways, the first-century equivalent of the electric chair, the punishment the empire used when it wanted to make an example of someone. Defy us, Rome said, and you can expect the same kind of pain and public humiliation.

So for Paul—a devout Jewish theologian and leader who was also a Roman citizen—it was unimaginable that God would redeem Israel, let alone the whole world, through someone who had been crucified. It turned everything Paul thought he knew about God upside down.

Like with the disciples, it changed everything.

Right; and it took Paul totally by surprise. And what really shocked him was that he came to see the cross not as this huge embarrassment but instead as the place where God shows up, completely unexpected, to reveal God's love and salvation not only for the people of Israel but for everyone.

Like in Mark's Gospel, at least the unexpectedness of it all, and like Luke's, in terms of it being for everyone.

Good memory.

So are you saying that the cross becomes a good thing for Paul, like in the different theories we looked at?

Great question. Maybe it would have been better if I said the cross was *both* a huge embarrassment *and also* the place where God shows up.

I'm not sure I'm following.

Well, for Paul the cross is always this awful, offensive thing. There's just no getting around that. At the same time, he sees it as the place where God's essential character, God's attitude toward God's people, is revealed most fully.

And that is . . . ?

That God loves us completely, fully, unconditionally, and eternally. And that God will do anything to draw us back to God in love. And that God forgives us . . . everything and always. And when I say "us," I mean *all* of us. Let's not forget that Jesus spent his life eating and drinking with sinners and outcasts and he hung on a cross surrounded by criminals. Again and again, God says that there's *no one* God cannot and will not love, even the people we might think don't deserve God's love.

That sounds really good, but it also sounds a lot like Abelard.

Well, we've said all along that each of the theories has some good parts as well as some not-so-great parts, and this is definitely what was good about Abelard's theory. But the point Paul is trying to make isn't that Jesus came to teach us about love, or to be an example for us. If he did, that would be just one more example of the law. The law is good, according to Paul, precisely because it tells us what is best for us. But the law doesn't save. It doesn't redeem. It can help to guide us in life, but it can't fix our relationship with God. It doesn't create *at-one-ment*.

So what does fix things?

Death and resurrection.

Well, I guess I assumed that. I mean, that's what we've been talking about this whole time, that Jesus' death and resurrection repairs our relationship with God. But how?

Actually, I was talking about *our* death and resurrection.

Okay, I didn't see that coming.

No problem—this can seem a little complicated. But sometimes I think that's because we *think* about it too much instead of just opening ourselves to *experiencing* it.

How do you mean?

Think back to how you felt when I said that I forgave you.

That's easy. I was really mad.

Why?

Like I said, I felt like you were judging me and I didn't see how you had the right to judge me.

What's so bad about being judged?

Well, I don't know; that's hard to say. I guess it just feels really bad. It's like you don't matter anymore, like someone has control over you, like you don't count, like someone else has all the power.

And that's because you felt like there wasn't anything you'd done to deserve that.

Absolutely. Although when I stop to think about it, I think that even if I had done something wrong I still wouldn't like it very much.

Why?

Well, most of the stuff we do in life we do because we feel like we have a good reason, even the things we do that hurt others. Obviously there are accidents, and we don't mind apologizing for those. But if a little kid takes his sister's toy, even if he knows it's wrong, he still kind of believes he deserves it and so should have it. So even though he knows he's wrong, when he's caught it still feels bad.

And judging from the newspapers and my own experience, I don't think we're all that different from kids. We do things for a reason, even harmful things. The reasons might not make sense to others, but they do to us. So we don't want to get caught. And even when we know something we've done is wrong, it's still really painful to be caught, to be judged, because all of a sudden it feels like we've been found unworthy, or suddenly we're not in control anymore.

Not in control how?

Not in control of what people think about you, not in control of what might happen to you, not in control of the future. We wonder, will this person like me, want to be in relationship with me, and so on. I think, on the whole, both for kids and adults, getting caught doing something wrong is one of the worst feelings in the world.

And this brings us back to Jesus.

It does?

Yeah. There's actually a Bible passage that describes just what you're talking about.

Let's hear it.

Okay, it begins with John 3:16.

Wait. I know that one. It was probably Abelard's favorite and certainly is mine: "For God so loved the world that he gave his only Son, so that everyone who believes in him may not perish but may have eternal life."

Great memory. But do you know how it continues?

Definitely not.

It goes on to say,

> Indeed, God did not send the Son into the world to condemn the world, but in order that the world might be saved through him. Those who believe in him are not condemned; but those who do not believe are condemned already, because they have not believed in the name of the only Son of God. And this is the judgment, that the light has come into the world, and people loved darkness rather than light because their deeds

*were evil. For all who do evil hate the light and do not come to the light,
so that their deeds may not be exposed. But those who do what is true
come to the light, so that it may be clearly seen that their deeds have been
done in God. (John 3:17-21)*

**Very interesting. The first part is all about God's great love for the world,
which I assume includes all of us. And that sounds fantastic. But the second
part is about what that great love sets in motion. It's about what actually *happens* because God loves us so much.**

Say a little more.

**Well, it's like what we said earlier: we hate the feeling of being judged. And
the interesting thing is, according to this passage, Jesus doesn't come to judge
us. Jesus actually comes to love us, but we feel judged and so run away.**

Why do you think we feel judged?

**I'd say it's like with Pat Nixon, or like what I felt earlier. Words of forgiveness, if you don't think you need them, are offensive. I mean, if you've done
something wrong and you want to hide it, then light is the last thing you
want. And if you've done something wrong but keep telling yourself it wasn't
that bad, or that you had a good reason, or that it wasn't really your fault, or
whatever, then forgiveness is the last thing you want, because it reminds you
that you did, in fact, do something that needs forgiving. It makes you feel out
of control.**

What about those times when we know we need to be forgiven?

**Then I suppose the words are the best ever. I mean, if I really have done something to hurt you, and I've gotten over all my excuses and can actually admit
it, then I'm probably worried about what it will have done to our friendship.
And then if I hear you say you forgive me, it's awesome because now I know
our relationship isn't over.**

Kind of like dying and being raised to life again.

**Ah, I think I see now what you meant when you said atonement isn't only
about Jesus' death and resurrection, but it's also about ours. Because if the
cross is the place where God reveals just how much God loves and forgives us,
then it's going to affect us in one of two ways. If we're not ready to admit that**

we need God's love and forgiveness, then it's going to feel like an accusation, like judgment, like dying. But if we get it—if we know we need God's love and forgiveness—then it'll be like being raised to new life.

Right. And it might even affect us both ways.

What do you mean?

Just that even if we get it, even if we know we need forgiveness and acceptance, we probably don't want to admit it at first.

I think that's true. Which also helps me see what you mean when you describe the cross and resurrection as events, even as experiences.

Say a little more.

Well, most of what we talked about with the other theories was an explanation—how the cross fits into some larger plan to take care of our problem. But when you talk about the cross and resurrection this way, it's more about actually experiencing something—namely, the judgment and death of being offered forgiveness when you don't think you need it, and the

new life that comes when you realize God really does forgive you, really does love you, and that your relationship is going to be okay. That feels to me like "doing atonement."

Right again. In a sense, God's love, embodied in Jesus' cross, does two things to us. First, it judges us.

Except, as we saw in John, the point isn't to judge us at all but to save us.

Right. So maybe better than talking about judgment, we should say that the first thing God's love does is to tell us the truth.

Like John's Gospel says, it's the light that shows us for what we are—lost, confused, insecure—basically, in need of God's love.

Right.

And that feels really bad. It puts to death all the illusions and dreams we have about ourselves, about being independent and in control and about being able to do everything on our own and not needing anyone. Yeah, that feels like death.

Which takes us back to the Gospel stories about Jesus.

How so?

When Jesus comes teaching and preaching and healing and feeding, he also comes forgiving. And so when people put Jesus on the cross, in John's words, it's their way of hating and fleeing the light.

I see. Except that they can't kill the light, because Jesus comes back.

He comes back. Which is why the resurrection is so important.

Kind of like in the ransom theory of atonement that we looked at first.

In a way. Jesus definitely enters into our life—the ups and downs, the challenges and struggles, the living and the dying. At the same time, it's not only in some kind of cosmic or mythical battle with evil, but also in a more down-to-earth way.

How so?

Because it's one thing for God to say I love and forgive you. But it's another for God to be able to do something about it.

What do you mean?

Well, God can talk about loving and forgiving us all God wants to, but in the end if we can just kill Jesus—God-made-flesh—and refuse the offer of forgiveness because it offends us, then nothing really changes.

I'm still not sure I'm following.

By raising Jesus from the dead, God shows that God's word of love and forgiveness is actually more powerful than death, more powerful than all our words of fear or insecurity or hate or of wanting to be in control or whatever.

So the cross may embody God's extreme love for us, but the resurrection is what shows us we can trust this love?

Yes. In a sense this is the second thing that Jesus' cross and resurrection does to us: it makes us, as you said earlier, come alive again. And it does this by telling us another truth.

Another truth?

Sure. If the cross and resurrection first tell us the truth about ourselves—that we're so afraid of being judged, that we'd rather reject love and forgiveness than admit our need and receive it—then they also tell us a second truth—that God simply won't rest until God has restored us, redeemed us, created *at-one-ment* with us.

So let me see if I've got it. When we see how much God loves us and wants to forgive us in and through Jesus' cross, we first find it difficult, even offensive, because we don't want to admit our need. But when we give up pretending that we're in control and give up our sense of independence, then we can hear God's words of love and forgiveness and receive them as what they are—promises of new life and restored relationship with God; in a word, atonement.

Very well put.

Thanks.

But all this leads me to another, and I think pretty big, question.

Shoot.

Well, this all sounds really good. That God loves and forgives us and all. But whatever happened to sin?

What do you mean? God forgives our sin.

But how can God just do that? Doesn't someone need to pay? Doesn't some- one need to make up for sin?

I didn't think I'd ever hear myself say this, but you're beginning to sound more than a little bit like Anselm.

I know, I know, and when we were talking about Anselm, I was the one who was asking why God can't just forgive us. But I think Anselm has gotten under my skin a bit. Or at least I can't quite forget his major concern about what happens to God's justice if God just goes and forgives people. I mean, why should anyone fear God or do what God wants if God doesn't back up the law with the threat of punishment?

This is a huge question, and obviously lots of Christians would agree with you, as they've embraced and adapted Anselm's theory into a pretty popular theory of atonement.

But let me start where you left off. Do you think that God's pri- mary purpose is to scare us or threaten punishment to get us to obey God's law?

Well, I don't like the way it sounds when you put it that way. But isn't that part of what punishment is for—not only to see that justice is done but also to make sure other people know that following the law—doing justice—is really important? I mean, that's true of laws the government makes for a whole country and rules parents make for their children. Don't you think?

I agree that one of the purposes of punishment is to warn people to follow the rules. But my question is whether you think that is God's *primary* purpose or activity. Or, let me try it this way: the threat of punishment, as we've both admitted, may indeed change our behav- ior, but does it change our hearts? Does it create new life?

What do you mean?

Well, let's say I want to do something bad, like break a law, but I don't because I'm afraid of being caught and punished. The threat of punishment may have made me think twice about breaking the law, but has it taken away my desire to break the law in the first place? Has it changed who I am? It may have made me afraid of doing something wrong, but has it made me *want* to do what is right?

No, I guess not.

I don't think so either. I do think, though, that God wants more from us than just a little better behavior. I think God wants to change our hearts. I think God wants us to actually *want* what is good for us and for our neighbors, not just consent to it because we're afraid of being punished. Fear of punishment doesn't really change us, but love does. Love, in fact, is the one thing that can empower us to be different than we're used to being.

Can you say a little more?

Sure. Plain and simple: change is hard. And I don't think you can ever change if you feel threatened. Oh, you can *act* like you've changed. But you can't really change. The only way you can risk changing is if you feel secure, if you feel accepted, if you feel loved.

And by loving us, God doesn't just give us an example but actually makes it possible for us to change?

Exactly.

Okay, that makes some sense, although it still sounds a lot like Abelard. I mean, even when I know I'm loved, I won't necessarily change. Then what?

Fair enough. But then we're back to the dynamic we talked about earlier with God's two truths. Maybe the point isn't change, but rather our dying and rising again by hearing the truths about who we are and who God is. And then any change that happens is a wonderful by-product, rather than the point. What matters, in the end, is that God loves us and will hold on to us no matter what. That's what Paul thought, anyway.

Really?

Yeah, in one of his letters he writes, "For I am convinced that neither death, nor life, nor angels, nor rulers, nor things present, nor things to come, nor powers, nor height, nor depth, nor anything else in all creation, will be able to separate us from the love of God in Christ Jesus our Lord" (Romans 8:38-39).

I'll admit that's pretty powerful. But what about the other questions? I mean, how can God just go and forgive us?

Because God's God.

Oh come on; I'm serious!

So am I. Let's go to Paul again. In the same chapter we just looked at he says:

> If God is for us, who is against us? He who did not withhold his own Son, but gave him up for all of us, will he not with him also give us everything else? Who will bring any charge against God's elect? It is God who justi-fies. Who is to condemn? It is Christ Jesus, who died, yes, who was raised, who is at the right hand of God, who indeed intercedes for us. Who will separate us from the love of Christ? (Romans 8:31-35)

Paul seems pretty adamant.

I agree. So that's the question: why can't God, who created the vast cosmos and still keeps things going, forgive us if God wants to?

I guess because it wouldn't be fair.

Fair to whom?

Fair to . . . well, fair to everyone who is obeying the law and following the rules.

And that would be . . .

Okay, so none of us really follow all the laws.
But it just seems like God ought to follow God's own rules about sin and punishment and all that.

And what rules are those?

Well, I don't know this stuff as well as you do, but doesn't the Bible say that the wages of sin are death and all of that?

Yes, and they are.

Well, there you go.

But we already die. People die from the dumb and foolish and awful and hurtful—that is, sinful—things they do all the time. Who says God has to carry out the sentence when we create so much misery for ourselves and each other all the time?

But what happens to divine justice?
I know, I know, I sound like Anselm again, but I think it's a good question.

It *is* a good question. And I think the Bible has a pretty good answer.

Great. I'd like to hear it.

It comes in the form of a parable that Jesus told, and it goes like this:

> For the kingdom of heaven is like a landowner who went out early in the morning to hire laborers for his vineyard. After agreeing with the laborers for the usual daily wage, he sent them into his vineyard. When he went out about nine o'clock, he saw others standing idle in the marketplace; and he said to them, "You also go into the vineyard, and I will pay you whatever is right." So they went. When he went out again about noon and about three o'clock, he did the same. And about five o'clock he went out and found others standing around; and he said to them, "Why are you standing here idle all day?" They said to him, "Because no one has hired us." He said to them, "You also go into the vineyard." When evening came, the owner of the vineyard said to his manager, "Call the laborers and give them their pay, beginning with the last and then going to the first." When those hired about five o'clock came, each of them received the usual daily wage. Now when the first came, they thought they would receive more; but each of them also received the usual daily wage. And when they received it, they grumbled against the landowner, saying, "These last worked only one hour, and you have made them equal to us who have borne the burden of the day and the scorching heat." But he replied to one of them, "Friend, I am doing you no wrong; did you not agree with me for the usual daily wage? Take what belongs to you and go; I choose to give to

this last the same as I give to you. Am I not allowed to do what I choose with what belongs to me? Or are you envious because I am generous?" So the last will be first, and the first will be last. (Matthew 20:1-16)

I think I see what you mean. It sounds like Jesus is saying that God's generosity will always surprise us, and sometimes even offend us.

I'm curious. Who in the parable did you identify with?

Well, I suppose I should have identified with the folks who showed up at the last hour. But, to be honest, I kind of identified with the ones who had been working all day. I mean, the story messes with our sense of fairness.

I think that's just what it does. And, believe me, I know what you mean. I think we assume we deserve what we get, so we sometimes begrudge others their good luck or good fortune. But this parable is definitely about God being, not unfair, but more than fair.

What do you mean?

Well, I agree with you that fairness is important. And it would definitely be unfair if God punished us for something we haven't done. But why can't God, as creator and judge of all, be more generous and merciful than we'd expect? Why can't God, when you come down to it, just forgive us?

But what about God's justice and honor and dignity and all that stuff Anselm brought up? What about the idea that God is a just king, and if a king doesn't punish unruly subjects, no one will keep the law?

I think you—and Anselm and all his followers for that matter— understand one thing very well but misunderstand another.

Okay, so let's start with the good part. What are we getting right?

I think what you're getting right is that the law is serious business. I mean, there's no doubt about it: we need to follow the law, and when we don't, things can go seriously awry. That's why God gives us the law in the first place, and why we're concerned with justice in the first place.

I'd agree with that. So, what are we missing?

That the law only reflects one dimension of our lives in this world. Law does matter . . . a lot. Most of us actually want good laws and good people to enforce just laws, even when it means we might get punished. Typically, that's because we want to be protected from the bad things others do, though in our better moments we realize that we need laws to protect others from some of the things we do.

Like when I'm pulled over for speeding. I may hate the fact that I just got a ticket, but when I calm down a bit and think about how many tens of thousands of people die in car crashes each year, I may recognize that what the troopers do is good, even when I'm the one being ticketed.

Right. We might call this the legal dimension of our lives.

But . . . ?

But there's another important dimension of our lives as well, and that has to do with relationships. And the law doesn't work quite so well when it comes to this dimension.

What do you mean?

Well, I think you actually got to the heart of this when you were critiquing Anselm. So like you said before—imagine running a family according to law. What would happen if parents counted up every wrong deed their children did and made sure their children paid for them? Or if children did the same for their parents?

Everyone would probably spend a lot of time punishing each other, and there wouldn't be much of a family left over.

Exactly. Or what if you dated according to the law, making sure to track every good and bad thing the person you were going out with did, and vice versa?

Your relationship wouldn't last that long.

Right again. And that's the relational dimension of our lives that is just as important, and maybe even more, than the legal dimension.

Don't get me wrong. The legal dimension matters a lot. After all, there are rules in families, and a person should pay attention if the person he or she is dating is behaving badly. But that isn't what holds a relationship together. What holds a relationship together is . . .

Love. And because of love, forgiveness. I think I get it. If we didn't forgive each other but expected every "sin" we do to each other to be tracked, recorded, and paid for, there'd be no relationship at all.

And I suspect that what God wants from us isn't just better behavior—though that's important—but a new and right relationship with God and each other. Paul talks a lot about righteousness, and we often think he means a kind of moral uprightness. But what the word really means is "right relationship," and that is something, as Paul learns, that law cannot achieve, but can only come from grace.

That helps a lot—to think that God definitely cares about law, about how we treat each other, but that fundamentally God cares even more about our relationship with God and with one another. Plus, as we said before, the best chance we have of changing, of actually following the rules and treating each other well, is not from the threat of punishment but from knowing that we are truly and deeply loved.

That's what I think Paul—and the rest of us—discover in the cross.

So God is not like the medieval king Anselm imagined?

In one respect God is like that kind of king, which is why God gives us laws and builds those laws into the fabric of creation—so that we really do reap what we sow. God cares deeply about how we treat each other and even gets disappointed or angry when we mistreat each other.

I've never seen my mom madder than when my sister and I were fighting. I mean, I had a great mom. She was very caring, but when one of us would bully the other, she'd get really upset.

That's a great analogy and helps us think a little differently about God's law and about God's anger. In terms of the law, it helps to remember that, at heart, there's a relational dimension even to the law; it's meant to help us get along with each other. When it comes to God's anger, it's important to recognize that it's always directed toward injustice in order to support and nurture the well-being of all the other people God loves so much.

So God does make laws, like a good king and, for that matter, like a good mom.

> Right. At the same time, though, God is even more like your mom than you might have imagined. Because, just like any loving parent, God knows that relationships—real, personal relationships—are created and nurtured not by fear or threat, but by love and forgiveness. No wonder that when Jesus taught his disciples to pray he had them say not, "Our King," but "Our Father."

Boy, this really does turn upside down what I used to think about God; kind of like you said happened with Paul.

> What do you mean?

Well, I'm so used to thinking about God as a lawgiver—kind of like Anselm, I guess—that it's hard to see God as a parent. Well, that's not quite right; I do think of God as a parent, but I guess it's usually as a pretty stern parent, a parent who loves me, to be sure, but is pretty keen on me keeping the rules.

But I'm still a little worried. If God is ultimately a parent who will stop at nothing to forgive us, a parent who loves us that much, can't that start to look a little pathetic? Isn't God worried about spoiling us? What happens to "tough love," for example?

> There's a parable about this, too.

Let's hear it.

> This one is about a father who had two sons. One of them asked his dad for his inheritance early. And when his dad gave him . . .

Wait, wait. I know this one. We even talked about it earlier, with regard to Abelard. It's the parable of the prodigal son.

> Right. From the Gospel of Luke (15:11-32).

And so when the father gives his son his share of the inheritance, the son wastes it all. And when the kid's down on his luck, he comes back to his father to ask forgiveness, but the father runs out to meet him and not only receives him back but throws a big party in his honor. This makes his older brother really mad, so his father goes out to talk with him, too. I can't quite remember how it all ends.

Great memory. And it actually ends right there, with us not knowing whether the older brother will join the party or not. A couple of details might help this parable sink in even more. First, there aren't trust funds in the first century. You usually only get an inheritance when someone dies, and so when his son asks him for his share . . .

It's like wishing his dad were dead. Yeah, that really stinks.

Also, a landowner like the one in the parable is really an important person. If we were going to tell it today, we might talk about him as the CEO of the major bank in town. People like this generally don't run. They have other people to run for them.

So when he runs out to meet his son . . .

He totally does something that most people would think is beneath him. I get it. In fact, it seems like he does this twice. Not only with the younger son but also with the older, when he leaves the party to invite him to come inside. I think I see where you're going with this. When it comes to the honor of a landowner, or a king for that matter, God is willing to chuck it all away because God is, at heart, a loving parent.

Right.

So God just forgives us.

Except that it's never "just forgives us," because that forgiveness does something to us.

That's right. It tells us the truth about ourselves, which puts to death all our dreams of making it on our own. It also tells us the truth about God, which raises us to new life because of God's promise of forgiveness and love. It turns out that promise is stronger than death. This is what makes us "at-one" with God.

Nicely put.

At the same time, though, it's also never "just forgives us," because it does something to God, too. Or, maybe better, costs God something.

What do you mean?

Like we said, Jesus goes to the cross because he "just forgave us." Remember when we talked about how forgiveness can be really offensive?

Are you kidding—I hated it when you told me that you forgave me.

Right, and that's what happens with Jesus. He makes people mad when he forgives them.

Like in John: they hate the light and so flee from it.

Right. But Jesus' forgiveness doesn't just offend individuals, it calls the whole system into question.

What system?

The system that says law is more important than love. The system that's all about accounting. The system that says "might makes right," that God can't just forgive someone, that is all about crime and punishment. The system—the legal system—that we live in.

But you yourself said that law is good.

It is good, but it's not the most important good. Jesus once fed people on the Sabbath, the holy day God appointed for rest when no one is supposed to work, and he was criticized for it. In response he said, "The sabbath was made for humankind, and not humankind for the sabbath" (Mark 2:27).

It sounds like what you said before, that even the law has a relational element.

That's exactly right. God is a God of relationship. From forming Adam and Eve from the ground, to establishing a covenant with the Israelites, to coming in the flesh to take on our life in Jesus, to forming the community of the Church, God is first and foremost interested in being in relationship with us.

Which is what atonement is all about.

But we forget that. We let the law, which itself was intended to promote right relationships, become more important than the relationships the law was intended to nurture. And so Jesus comes proclaiming the kingdom of God, a kingdom and rule that is just plain different than the one we've become accustomed to, and he demonstrates that different kingdom in word and deed.

How do you mean?

We live in a world where only some people are fed, and so Jesus feeds the hungry. We live in a world where people are sick and die needlessly, and so Jesus heals them. We live in a world where strength is honored over compassion, where wealth is the measure of importance rather than integrity, where power is measured by what you can destroy rather than what you can create, and so every act of grace, every sign or miracle of compassion, every act of healing, every time Jesus embraces someone the system has declared an outcast, he is calling the whole system into question.

And they kill him for it. More than that, they make an example of him, of what happens when you call the powers that be into question.

Yes they do. And we do, too.

We do? I wasn't even there.

But we still participate in this system of laws that has gotten out of hand, overreached itself, that serves itself rather than the right relationships that are so important to God. And each time we realize that—each time God reaches out to us in in forgiveness, which is also judgment—we want to run and flee all over again. As much as I'd like to think otherwise, I just don't think most of us would do any different if Jesus came among us again. The Gospel stories, in the end, aren't really about the Jews or the Romans crucifying Jesus; they're about telling us the truth that all of us participate in a system that crucified Jesus, because he called us back to right relationship with God and each other.

So, confessing our failure and need, and becoming dependent on God's grace and mercy—that's dying.

That's dying.

But, just like in the Gospel stories, it doesn't end there. Death doesn't have the last word.

No, it doesn't. Jesus doesn't stay dead, and neither do we. Because once we realize what state we're in—or to put it in the terms we've used before, once we hear the first truth the cross tells us—we can hear and believe the second truth that God has loved us all along and desired life for us all along.

And that's being raised again.

Yes, it is.

So that's "doing atonement."

That's "doing atonement."

I like it.

Most of time, that is. I mean, facing the truth that something in me needs to die is hard. But it's worth it, because I'd rather have the truth than a neat theory or nice story. And it seems like it's only after I feel like I'm dying that I feel truly alive again.

I couldn't agree more. Which is a good thing, because it never ends.

What do you mean?

That's the thing about this experience of cross and resurrection. It's not like the theories that you can take on and off the shelf when you want them. Because we're human, we're caught up in this ongoing cycle of dying and rising. Martin Luther, in fact, said this is what happens every day as we hear God's Word and come to faith anew.

It really never ends?

Not as long as this life lasts, at least. We are human, very human, and so we always fall short. Yet we are those humans that God loves so very much. We are the humans Christ died for.

Like I said, this is pretty different than I'd imagined God to be. I mean, this God is so—I don't know—loving, to be sure, but also really vulnerable, even weak. Is that what you meant earlier when you said that the cross forces us to think differently about how we understand God's power?

That's exactly right. We tend to think of power as the ability to do something, to create something, or, more often, the ability to destroy something—to take life, to win wars, and so on. But in the cross God redeems the world not through conquest but through vulnerability, and not through war but through forgiveness. God, in short, is strong through weakness.

Maybe that's why the apostle Paul calls this whole cross thing foolishness and a stumbling block. I mean, it's just not what you expect and totally messes with your ideas of what power is.

Maybe another movie example would help.

I'm game.

Have you seen *Schindler's List*?

Sure. It's about the guy who saved a large number of Jewish persons during World War II. It's been a little while, but I remember how powerful it was.

Do you remember the commandant who oversees the work at Schindler's factory?

Definitely. He was awful. Killing people for any little infraction of the rules and sometimes for nothing at all. He just wanted to kill them, I think, to show off his power and keep them afraid of him.

I think you're right. And then one day Schindler says to him, "Power is when we have every justification to kill, and we don't." But the commandant doesn't believe him. He just can't imagine that's true, so Schindler continues, "That's what the emperors had. A man stole something, he's brought in before the emperor, he throws himself down on the ground, and he begs for mercy. He knows he's going to die. And the emperor . . . pardons him."

The power to forgive rather than kill, even in the name of justice. I remember that. A little later, doesn't the commandant try that, too?

Yes. He even practices on his own, in front of the mirror, but ultimately he's can't pull it off.

He's not powerful enough to forgive, only to kill.

But God forgives. As Paul says, "God proves God's righteousness by justifying" — that is, forgiving—"the one who has faith in Jesus"

(Romans 3:26) And in what God actually did—forgive and justify us—we discover what power is, and what justice is, and who God is.

God is the one who is strong enough to forgive. That sounds good, really good. But it also raises another question for me. What happens to the idea of sacrifice? When you said the Jesus died for us, that reminded me of all this.

That's a great question. I think we can still talk about Jesus as making a sacrifice. But instead of talking about *who* the sacrifice was made *to*, we might shift the discussion to the question: *for whom* was the sacrifice made?

Hmmm. I'm not sure I've followed that.

Most talk about sacrifice is about God—Jesus needed to be sacrificed to God to satisfy God's need for punishment. But I want to say that what matters isn't the "to whom," but instead the "for whom." Jesus made the sacrifice for us because God loves us.

Any chance you could provide an example?

Sure. Let's go back to the sacrifice Harry Potter's mother made for him. Who did she make it to?

Now that you mention it, I actually have no idea. I mean, Voldemort killed her, but I wouldn't want to say she sacrificed herself *to* him. So I don't know.

That's right. In fact, the question seems beside the point. But *for whom* did Lily Potter make her sacrifice?

That's easy. She did it for Harry, the son she loved so much. And that sacrifice had power.

That's right. The whole series turns on the power of love to . . . well, redeem.

I've never thought of it that way, but that helps me recognize that the whole point of the cross isn't *who* Jesus is making a sacrifice to—an angry or holy or just God—but rather *for whom* Jesus is dying. Us! Because God loves us.

Exactly right.

Very cool.

One more question?

Only one?!

Well, how about for now, at least one more.

Sure; shoot.

As long as we're talking about dying, don't we have to ask again about this question of violence? I mean, you said earlier that one of the dangers of Anselm's theory is that it may unintentionally glorify violence, whether it's the violence you do or that happens to you. Well, what's different about this? Jesus still achieves atonement through violence.

I'm not sure that he does. When we talked about Anselm, we had this sense that Jesus had to die because it's all part of some larger plan.

And you don't think Jesus had to die?

Actually, I do. That's what the Gospels seem to be saying, but I'm not sure it's because of some plan.

Say more.

Jesus has to die because that's what happens to people like Jesus in this world, in this system of law and justice that is threatened by forgiveness. It's kind of like when you put a guy who goes around forgiving others and proclaiming God's kingdom of love in this kind of world, ninety-nine times out of a hundred . . .

He's going to get killed. Except that we should make that one hundred times out of a hundred.

Right.

So Jesus doesn't glorify violence.

In fact, his death at the hands of a violent world, empire, and system of "justice" calls the whole order, and our all-too-eager use of violence to achieve good ends into question. And at the same time his resurrection promises another way—God's way, in God's own good time.

I like that. A lot. But is that it, then?

What do you mean?

Well, I think I finally have a pretty good grasp on the cross. Or maybe I should say, I think the cross has a pretty good grasp on me. So I'm wondering if that's all there is to talk about. Have we gotten to the end?

Good heavens, no! In some ways it's just the beginning.

Say that again?

In some ways it's just the beginning. One way to think about all of our cross-and-resurrection talk is to see it as a way of figuring out God and, in particular, figuring out how the cross fits into God's plan and all that. I think we've moved beyond that by stressing how the cross and resurrection aren't just theories but are actual events, experiences we have in the presence of the living and loving God.

But the next mistake would be to imagine that it all ends with the cross and resurrection, even with the life-and-death experience of cross and resurrection we've been talking about.

Can you say a little more?

Once you know yourself to be a person that God loves this much, then your whole outlook on life changes.

I'm still not sure I'm following you.

Well, as Paul writes, "If God is for us, who is against us?" (Romans 8:31). Or, to put it another way, once you know how much God loves you—think, the cross—and once you realize that God has defeated death and joined you to that victory—think, resurrection—then there's not a whole lot left to be afraid of.

Actually, that's not totally fair. There are, I suppose, still things to be afraid of, but knowing that you have God's promise of love and life creates courage in us to face the things we fear in faith.

So the cross and resurrection, in a sense, set us free.

Right. Free to be the people God created us to be. Free to love, forgive, and care for others because we've been loved, forgiven, and taken care of. Free to model our lives after Jesus, standing up for the people left behind by the system that values law over the relationship, and free to remind everyone we meet that God's kingdom is different.

Again, this sounds a bit like Abelard.

It does in that we can see Jesus' whole life as an example. But the point isn't that we're trying to become more lovable. The point is that, knowing we are loved this much, we're free to love others in return. Yes, we'll fall short, even fail. But that's part of the point, too. We will fall short—die—but be raised once again, and try again.

And we just keep doing that?

Until Christ comes again. That's part of the promise, as well. That eventually, God will come in Jesus to establish this kingdom of love and right relationship, and we won't even need the law anymore. Until then, though, we live in hope, striving and falling short, confessing and receiving forgiveness, dying and being raised to new life once again.

You know, at first I thought that sounded a little hopeless, or at least redundant. But now I think it actually sounds kind of courageous. That because of the cross and resurrection, we can hang in there and make a difference,

trusting that the God who raised Jesus will redeem us and, eventually, all the world.

That's right. That's the freedom of living in light of the cross and resurrection not as a theory that tries to explain Jesus' life in light of a failed system but instead helps us imagine a new system all together and, not only imagine it, but participate in it.

Which is kind of an awesome invitation.

Yeah, it really is. The apostle Paul actually says that once God has reconciled us to God—and for Paul, it's always *we* who need to be reconciled, not God—God actually entrusts us with what he calls the "ministry of reconciliation" (2 Corinthians 5:18).

So that's what you mean by saying it's just the beginning.

Right. All we've talked about is really, really important. And it doesn't happen just once. Our whole lives long we'll experience the dying and rising we're talking about. But all that sets us free for life in God's world, for living and loving others in God's name.

Sort of like we become a community of atonement.

I like that. At our best, we are indeed a community of atonement.

Very cool. This all really does make sense, not just in theory, but also in the way it affects me.
Speaking of theories, though, I think it would help me to review the questions we put to the other three ways of making sense of the cross.

Sounds like a good idea.

Well, in terms of what the problem is, I think it's very similar to the other three. We are trapped in sin and death, as in the classic theory. We definitely can't dig ourselves out of the hole we're in, with Anselm. And we really do need to love each other better, with Abelard. But it's also bigger. That is, it seems now like our whole way of relating to each other—actually our whole way of being in the world—is off kilter. I think that's what we meant when we said that Jesus calls the whole system into question.

At one point the apostle Paul says that the whole creation longs to be set free (Romans 8:19-23).

Yeah, that sums it up.

Second question?

Well, in terms of what fixes things, it's about what God does in Jesus, again like with the other three. But it's also about what *happens* to us because of Jesus. That is, it's not like God is doing some deal off to the side—paying off the devil or paying back our debt for us. Instead, the cross and resurrection, as we said, put us to death and then raise us to life again. It's that the problem is almost too big to fix. God has to start over, in a way, by not just tinkering with the larger system, but by creating a new one.

> Sometimes I think that's what Jesus means when he says, "I am the way, the truth, and the life. No one comes to the Father except through me" (John 14:6). Jesus died and was raised again. That's what we need to do, too, except we can't on our own, and so God comes to us in the two truths of the cross and resurrection to make it happen.

To move to the third question, this paints a very different picture of God and ourselves. God is steadfastly loving but also determined to redeem us, even to the point of becoming human and taking on our lot and our life and dying.

> Right. And God's power ends up being revealed most fully in God's vulnerability. That is, God shows up just where you'd least expect God to be.

Which is good news, because the places you'd expect God to be we'll probably never make it to! But instead, God comes down to us, and all of a sudden we discover that, no matter what we've done or had done to us, we're those people God loves, those people Jesus died for, those people God is committed to redeem, raise up, and set loose in the world to care for each other and share this good news.

> I like the way you've put that.

Thanks. And all of that, to get to our fourth question, brings us to a different picture of the Christian life.

> Actually, in some ways it's very much the same picture as you find all over the New Testament: we're called to live and love as Jesus did—not because we have to, but because we can. If God is for us, to

borrow from Paul, then we're free to love each other, to take chances, to risk ourselves, to care for those around us. We become, as you said, a community of atonement.

I'm actually eager to see just what this life and community look like. I'm not sure what I'll find, but I'm pretty sure God will be there.

God will be there loving, forgiving, sustaining, creating, and even recreating. And the incredible part is, God invites us all to be part of it.

That is pretty incredible.

So, I guess now we're done—well, not done, just beginning, actually—but maybe done talking for now. Thank you. I've appreciated our conversation.

I have, too. Your questions and insights have helped me understand what God is doing—both through Jesus and through us—better. So maybe we should, if not end, at least conclude this part of our conversation with the words some Christians say at the end of their worship services: Go in peace and serve the Lord.

Thanks be to God.

Insights and Questions

For Further Reading

Aulén, Gustaf. *Christus Victor*. S.P.C.K. Publishing, 1970.

Brown, Raymond. *Death of the Messiah: From Gethsemane to the Grave* in Anchor Bible Reference Library. New York: Doubleday, 1994.

Carroll, John T. and Green, Joel B. *The Death of Jesus in Early Christianity*. Grand Rapids: Baker Academic, 2007.

Forde, Gerhard O. *Where God Meets Man*. Minneapolis: Augsburg Books, 1972.

Green, Joel B. and Baker, Mark D. *Recovering the Scandal of the Cross: Atonement in New Testament & Contemporary Contexts*. Downers Grove, IL: IVP Academic, 2011.

McKnight, Scott. *A Community Called Atonement*. Nashville: Abingdon Press, 2007.

Philip Ruge-Jones. *The Word of the Cross in a World of Glory*. Augsburg Fortress, 2008.

Schmeichen, Peter. *Saving Power: Theories of Atonement and Forms of the Church*. Grand Rapids: Wm. P. Eerdmans, 2005.

Trelstad, Marit. *Cross Examinations: Readings on the Meaning of the Cross*. Minneapolis: Fortress Press, 2006.

Weaver, J. Denny. *The Nonviolent Atonement*. Grand Rapids: Wm. B. Eerdmans, 2001.

Westhelle, Vitor. *The Scandalous God: The Use and Abuse of the Cross*. Minneapolis: Fortress Press, 2007.

Wright, N. T. *Christians at the Cross: Finding Hope in the Passion, Death, and Resurrection of Jesus*. Word Among Us Press, 2008.